SHAKESPEARE'S ENGLAND

There are a number of HORIZON CARAVEL BOOKS
published each year. Titles now available are:

PHARAOHS OF EGYPT
LEONARDO DA VINCI
THE FRENCH REVOLUTION
CORTES AND THE AZTEC CONQUEST
CAESAR.
THE UNIVERSE OF GALILEO AND NEWTON
THE VIKINGS
MARCO POLO'S ADVENTURES IN CHINA
SHAKESPEARE'S ENGLAND

CAPTAIN COOK AND THE SOUTH PACIFIC
THE SEARCH FOR EARLY MAN
JOAN OF ARC
EXPLORATION OF AFRICA
NELSON AND THE AGE OF FIGHTING SAIL
ALEXANDER THE GREAT
RUSSIA UNDER THE CZARS
HEROES OF POLAR EXPLORATION
KNIGHTS OF THE CRUSADES

American Heritage also publishes AMERICAN HERITAGE JUNIOR LIBRARY
books, a similar series on American history. The titles now available are:

JAMESTOWN: FIRST ENGLISH COLONY
AMERICANS IN SPACE
ABRAHAM LINCOLN IN PEACE AND WAR
AIR WAR AGAINST HITLER'S GERMANY
IRONCLADS OF THE CIVIL WAR
THE ERIE CANAL
THE MANY WORLDS OF BENJAMIN FRANKLIN
COMMODORE PERRY IN JAPAN
THE BATTLE OF GETTYSBURG
ANDREW JACKSON, SOLDIER AND STATESMAN
ADVENTURES IN THE WILDERNESS
LEXINGTON, CONCORD AND BUNKER HILL
CLIPPER SHIPS AND CAPTAINS
D-DAY, THE INVASION OF EUROPE
WESTWARD ON THE OREGON TRAIL
THE STORY OF YANKEE WHALING

THE FRENCH AND INDIAN WARS
GREAT DAYS OF THE CIRCUS
STEAMBOATS ON THE MISSISSIPPI
COWBOYS AND CATTLE COUNTRY
TEXAS AND THE WAR WITH MEXICO
THE PILGRIMS AND PLYMOUTH COLONY
THE CALIFORNIA GOLD RUSH
PIRATES OF THE SPANISH MAIN
TRAPPERS AND MOUNTAIN MEN
MEN OF SCIENCE AND INVENTION
NAVAL BATTLES AND HEROES
THOMAS JEFFERSON AND HIS WORLD
DISCOVERERS OF THE NEW WORLD
RAILROADS IN THE DAYS OF STEAM
INDIANS OF THE PLAINS

COVER: *A bust of Shakespeare is seen against the panorama of seventeenth-century London.*
BUST COURTESY THE FOLGER SHAKESPEARE LIBRARY
FRONT ENDSHEET: *Shakespeare is surrounded by his contemporaries in this detail from a painting. Jonson sits at his elbow; Raleigh (hatted) and Southampton stand on the right.*
IN THE COLLECTION OF THE CORCORAN GALLERY OF ART
BACK ENDSHEET: *This engraving is a detail from the broad view of London that is used as background on the cover. The original engraving is by a Dutch artist named Visscher.*
PERMISSION OF THE TRUSTEES OF THE BRITISH MUSEUM
TITLE PAGE: *The Globe Theatre and a bear-baiting ring are also from Visscher's London.*
PERMISSION OF THE TRUSTEES OF THE BRITISH MUSEUM

A HORIZON CARAVEL BOOK

SHAKESPEARE'S ENGLAND

By the Editors of
HORIZON MAGAZINE

In Consultation with
LOUIS B. WRIGHT
Director, The Folger Shakespeare Library

ILLUSTRATED WITH PAINTINGS, DRAWINGS,
AND ENGRAVINGS OF THE PERIOD

Published by American Heritage Publishing Co., Inc.
Book Trade and Institutional Distribution by
Harper & Row

SECOND EDITION
Library of Congress Catalogue Card Number: 64–12231

1408

FOREWORD

When William Shakespeare was about twenty, his life changed radically. Some accounts say he was caught stealing a deer from the estate of a local nobleman, and that poaching was the reason for his leaving home. Modern scholars reject the tale but agree that something crucial happened at that time: Shakespeare, the man who was to become the world's greatest playwright, left Stratford and walked to London, whatever his reason.

The purpose of this book is not to challenge the debatable points of Shakespeare's biography or to probe his literary reputation. It is, rather, to present the playwright as a man of his day against the colorful tapestry of his England, the kingdom under Elizabeth I and James I. In the reigns of those monarchs the nation was emerging from centuries of medieval turmoil. The small island that had changed so little since the Norman Conquest of 1066 suddenly became a center of international adventure, political experimentation, and artistic development.

Young Shakespeare was fortunate to be in England, and in London, when he was. The first professional theatre opened in the capital in 1576; he arrived, stage-struck and in search of a job, around 1587. He retired to Stratford as a wealthy gentleman in 1611, only a generation before the theatres of England were closed by the Puritans. During Shakespeare's London years, England seethed with plots and intrigue and throbbed with pageantry; everywhere a writer looked there was a scene to fire his imagination. Like Sir Walter Raleigh and other daring contemporaries, William Shakespeare was indeed an Elizabethan who took advantage of his time.

With the story of Shakespeare's England this book presents many contemporary illustrations, lively drawings and woodcuts, as well as more formal paintings and portraits. In these may be seen an age whose spectacular flowering is still yielding great benefits to new generations throughout the world.

THE EDITORS

6

This view of an Elizabethan wedding feast was painted about 1590, shortly after Shakespeare came to London. From the right, the wedding party arrives at the feast, preceded by bakers, violinists, and a gentleman brandishing a bouquet. In the background (at left) the grim Tower of London can be seen, a reminder that all was not merry in Shakespeare's England.

7

In the Poets' Corner of Westminster Abbey is a statue of Shakespeare designed by William Kent.

The Cloud capt Towers
The Gorgeous Palaces
The Solemn Temples
The Great Globe itself
Yea all which it Inherit,
Shall Dissolve
And like this Insubstantial Vision
Leave not a wreck behind

GVL: KENT INV:

8

CONTENTS

I

Some houses in Stratford, with their projecting second stories and small windows, are medieval and still look much as they did in Shakespeare's day.

THE BRIDGE TO STRATFORD

Elizabeth I, England's greatest queen, had but a short time to live. She left her London residence at Whitehall after Christmas, 1602, and made the brief river journey to Richmond Palace. She arrived in the midst of a chilling January downpour, and there she waited, her remarkable mind perfectly aware of her failing health, her sharp glance missing nothing.

Some great monarchs of history have chosen to die with the treasures of their kingdoms piled high about them. But Elizabeth commanded a distinguished company of players to come and entertain her—the Lord Chamberlain's Men. They arrived at the palace gates in February, 1603, a troupe of perhaps six well-known actors and their assistants. At one end of a lofty hall they set up their platform stage, the musicians sounded a flourish, and the brilliantly costumed Queen feasted her eyes on a dramatic spectacle for the last time. A few weeks later she died, and an era ended.

William Shakespeare was a senior member of the Lord Chamberlain's Men. He was fully aware of the honor Elizabeth had bestowed on his troupe at Richmond, and on many previous occasions. Not yet forty, he had risen to prominence in the preceding decade and would live to enjoy new triumphs in the decade ahead. As London's bells tolled the sad news of the Queen's death, he must have considered how many blessings her reign had brought him. And perhaps sharp memories flashed through his mind: his childhood in Stratford, his early days as a newcomer to London, the building of the famous Globe Theatre (of which he was now a part owner), his lively contacts with all manner of men and women.

It is possible for writers today to recreate these scenes from the past with some accuracy, thanks to 350 years of Shakespearean scholarship and tradition. However, what Shakespeare felt or how he conducted himself in each scene is somewhat more difficult to determine. For the basic materials are sparse. There are legal papers such as his marriage license and his will, the records of his children's baptism, a few mentions of his professional skills in the writings of others, and information carved on his tombstone. There are also old biographies, but none of them yield much more information than the musty records themselves.

The first attempt to put the known events of Shakespeare's life in order was published in 1662, forty-six years after his death. A clergyman named Thomas Fuller included Shakespeare in a collection of biographies of "worthy" Englishmen. Although Fuller's account was heavily padded with irrelevant material, it was at least conscientious. The author was not sure of the date of Shakespeare's death, and he left a blank so the information could be filled in subsequently.

Later in the seventeenth century there were two other major attempts to chronicle Shakespeare's life, but these manuscripts were never published. The next published biography did not appear until 1709. It was written by Nicholas Rowe to accompany a six-volume edition of

The Shakespeare house on Henley Street was restored after it became government property in 1847. The playwright's bedroom, shown below, is furnished now as it may have been at the time he used it.

Shakespeare's mother was born in the tiny farm village of Wilmcote, four miles northwest of Stratford.

Shakespeare's plays. Although the Rowe biography was brief and to the point, it contained much inaccurate information; it was based mainly on stories the author had heard and not on contemporary accounts. By Rowe's time, everyone who had known Shakespeare or who had had any firsthand knowledge of him was dead.

Some biographers have tried to make up for this lack of contemporary material by looking for hints about Shakespeare's life and personality in his writings. Others, frustrated by the lack of evidence, have dared suggest that Shakespeare's works were written by someone else. Nevertheless, from certain biographies and from scholarly writings, enough knowledge can be gleaned to yield many vivid images of Shakespeare and his England as he rose to prominence—and then to greatness—in the theatre.

The first professional acting company to begin making regular visits to Stratford rode into town on a summer's day in 1568. The men had come over the dusty road from London—some on foot, some on horseback—with their costumes, props, and musical instruments trundling along in a wagon behind them. Without pause they rumbled over Clopton Bridge, the sound of their horses' hoofs and the wagon wheels echoing hollowly from beneath the stone arches. Then the troupe slowed their pace, for Bridge Street was a busy thoroughfare. There, in addition to the children flocking to greet the newcomers, were the tradesmen—bakers, cobblers, smiths—whose shops lined the street and whose wares were often displayed on tables in the town square.

14

After proceeding to the town hall, the actors were welcomed officially by the mayor, or high bailiff, as he was called then. The man who bore this title in 1568 was John Shakespeare, father of the playwright. An ambitious and successful man, John Shakespeare wore his scarlet, fur-trimmed robe with the dignity of a nobleman, but he was not an aristocrat. He had reached Stratford's highest office by being as forceful and businesslike in civic affairs as he was in his own trade of glovemaking. His rise to posts of prominence had also been helped by his marriage to Mary Arden, daughter of a prosperous landowner in nearby Wilmcote.

Touring players needed the sanction of civic officials before they could perform in a town. Thus a theatrical performance in Stratford took place first in the town hall's main room—a long, narrow chamber with a scaffold set up at one end to serve as a stage platform. The trial performance that was given in this chamber was free to as many persons as could be squeezed in, for the actors would be paid by the town council. No doubt John Shakespeare had the best seat in the room, for he was the town's most important official. And his son William, who was four at the time, may have been with him.

TEXT CONTINUED ON PAGE 19

Engravings on these pages depict two types of theatrical performances that Stratfordians could attend. Above, touring actors try out for the town's high bailiff. At left, a mystery play is acted in nearby Coventry. In a scene from the life of Christ, Pilate, on the wagon stage, washes his hands.

15

SHAKESPEARE'S ENGLAND

In 1587 at Fotheringhay Castle, Queen Elizabeth's cousin and rival, Mary Queen of Scots, was beheaded. A year later, the famous Spanish Armada, which had been dispatched against England partly because of Mary's execution, was defeated in the English Channel. It was at that time that William Shakespeare, an impressionable and restless young man, left Warwickshire and the happy associations of Stratford (see detailed map below), and trudged to London. To him it must have seemed as if all England were a stage on which historic and bloody events were being enacted; thus it is not surprising that when the Globe Theatre in which he was part owner was built in 1599, the Latin motto over the door was "All the world's a stage." Yet as the sixteenth century drew to a close, the events of Shakespeare's own theatre life—the provincial tours and court performances—became nearly as important to the development of English culture as any rebellion or conflict of the past.

Irish Rebellion
1597

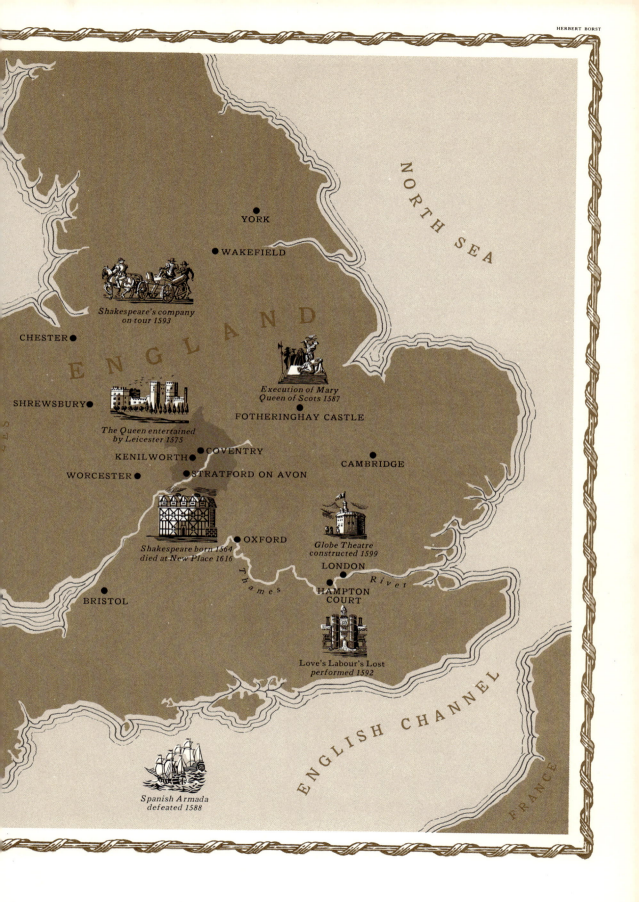

NORTH SEA

ENGLAND

YORK

WAKEFIELD

*Shakespeare's company
on tour 1593*

CHESTER

*Execution of Mary
Queen of Scots 1587*

SHREWSBURY

FOTHERINGHAY CASTLE

*The Queen entertained
by Leicester 1575*

KENILWORTH   COVENTRY

WORCESTER   STRATFORD ON AVON   CAMBRIDGE

*Shakespeare born 1564
died at New Place 1616*

OXFORD

*Globe Theatre
constructed 1599*

LONDON

Thames   River

HAMPTON
COURT

BRISTOL

*Love's Labour's Lost
performed 1592*

ENGLISH CHANNEL

FRANCE

*Spanish Armada
defeated 1588*

The joy of drinking ale outside an English tavern was often enlivened by the songs of a minstrel troupe.

TEXT CONTINUED FROM PAGE 15

Most of the plays brought to towns and cities in provincial England were full of moral preachments and lessons in righteousness. No doubt the meaning of these plays was beyond the ken of young Shakespeare and other Stratford children. But if the young people missed the point of a play, they were probably stirred by its physical action and its success as an exercise in make-believe.

Provincial theatre left much to the imagination of its audience. There were no lighting or scenic effects, few props, and none of the trappings that were later used to suggest real surroundings. The acting was vigorous, and it tended to be exaggerated instead of realistic. Performers relied mainly on the volume and pitch of their voices to convey youth or age, virtue or wickedness.

The touring companies were small, well-practiced groups of six or seven actors each. These men were usually so versatile, and so adept at making quick changes, that they could easily present a play of many characters. The actors learned to play more than one role in a single performance, but only the leading actors in a company had a choice of parts. The major roles in the popular dramas of the day were passionate and violent. Mad scenes and murders were frequent, and they were not played with restraint. A bladder of animal blood might be concealed in the actor's costume, to spurt forth at the critical moment in an axing or a stabbing.

The players who came to Stratford on that day in 1568 were no doubt masters of this trick, and of many others. Their trial performance was successful; they received their license from the high bailiff and then moved to one of the local inns to prepare a performance for the following day. Their scaffold stage had to be set up at one end of the rectangular innyard. Most of the spectators would stand on the ground below the platform, but the more prosperous members of the audience would sit on balconies outside the upstairs rooms that overlooked the yard. There, in the light of an afternoon sun, the playgoers of Stratford could watch as vast battles were fought, rogues were decapitated, and men were turned into animals by the magic of the theatre.

Violence was an essential ingredient of sixteenth-century theatre; violence for the sake of violence, violence to emphasize lofty themes. And nearly all plays had something important to say. In this respect the plays owed much to their theatrical predecessors, the mystery plays of medieval times. These plays, which dramatized episodes from the Bible, were performed throughout the Middle Ages on

Sixteenth-century England was not alone in its love of entertainment. Europeans were eager fairgoers, as can be seen in this painting by Pieter Brueghel. In the center of the gaiety below, unnoticed by all but a few of the revelers, some actors perform on an outdoor stage.

religious holidays and at sacred festivals. Mystery plays were not acted by professionals, but by the town craftsmen, who were organized into guilds. At first, the performances took place inside churches, later on platforms just outside. Eventually, the plays were staged on movable, flat-bed wagons called pageants and were seen in the streets of various market towns.

Just as the content of plays was changing by the time Shakespeare was born, so were the places of presentation—from the church to the street to the innyard. And the players were no longer amateurs but professionals, formed into companies, who made their living by no other craft.

After the summer of 1568, the touring players came to Stratford every year, and eventually twice a year. No doubt young Shakespeare saw many performances, and very possibly he visited Coventry, twenty miles from his home, to see the annual mystery play revivals that were staged each year before a huge crowd of neighboring townfolk. When Shakespeare was twelve, the acting companies of both the Earl of Warwick and the Earl of Worcester came to Stratford, and a year later a distinguished acting company under the patronage of the Earl of Leicester came to town.

To protect themselves from persecution by city and town authorities—many of whom had puritanical leanings and held all actors in disrepute—acting companies sought

Kenilworth, a majestic feature of England's landscape since Norman times, was Elizabeth's gift to her favorite, the Earl of Leicester.

the patronage of noblemen. In exchange for their patronage and protection, these noblemen enjoyed private performances in the great halls of their homes.

In 1572 city authorities in London issued an edict that threatened to snuff out touring companies like those that came to Stratford. By the terms of this edict, only actors who were the actual servants of a nobleman could go on tour. To counter the ban, members of the Earl of Leicester's company sent a letter to their patron with an urgent plea. They requested his "license to certify that we are your household servants when we shall have occasion to travel amongst our friends, as we do usually once a year and as other noblemen's players do." The request was granted. The actors were free to go on tour.

Leicester was a powerful and magnificent nobleman; he was also the Queen's favorite. In the summer of 1575, when Shakespeare was eleven, Elizabeth and her entourage descended upon Leicester's country home at Kenilworth. The castle, which was begun in the twelfth century, stood just fifteen miles across the fields from Stratford. The performances put on at Kenilworth for the Queen's amusement were so spectacular that talk of them must have created considerable excitement in neighboring Stratford. It is often suggested that William Shakespeare and other boys of the town, attracted by the stories they had heard

and by the cannon salvos and the fireworks displays, became admiring spectators of many of the open-air performances that so delighted the Queen. To have attended these spectacles at night would have been difficult, however, for Stratford's summer curfew was at 8:00 P.M. A visit to Kenilworth would have been equally difficult by day because of the demands on young people to attend school.

From the time they were seven until they were twelve or thirteen, the pupils of the King's New School in Stratford spent their weekdays, summer and winter, in school. They were drilled extensively in Latin and introduced to Greek. The school day lasted from seven in the morning until five in the afternoon, with two hours off for the usual midday meal at home.

Soon after Shakespeare's twelfth birthday in 1576, his father's career took a downward turn. John Shakespeare ceased attending meetings of the Stratford town council, and for an unknown reason, eventually withdrew from public life. Whereas he was once a prosperous merchant, he was now forced to live off the sale, leasing, and mortgaging of much of his wife's property.

Like any other civic official, John Shakespeare had probably enjoyed the respect and deference accorded him by the town's leading citizens. He had aspired to become a member of the gentry when he achieved prominence and had applied for a coat of arms. For some reason—perhaps because of his decline—the escutcheon was not awarded.

Times were hard now for the Shakespeare family, and William undoubtedly had to give up his formal schooling—possibly before he was thirteen. Some biographers have claimed that young Shakespeare was later arrested for stealing deer, or that he became a butcher's apprentice, but these are probably fictional notions. It seems likely that he may have helped his father for a time in the glove-making trade—doing errands and odd jobs, perhaps dressing skins. He may have served England as a soldier in the Low Countries or taught school in a town near Stratford. But there is no proof of either activity.

Although most of his early life is obscure, it is known that he married in 1582, when he was eighteen. His bride, eight years his senior, was Anne Hathaway, daughter of a

A woodcut titled "Boys Will Be Boys" (above) depicts classroom prankishness in Shakespeare's day. His school was in the building attached to the Guild Chapel (above, right). The house where he was born is at right.

BOTH: BRITISH INFORMATION SERVICES

What is known of Shakespeare's family life comes mostly from documents referring to his children. His son died in 1596, and according to records (left) was buried in Stratford on August 11.

Scenes from a sumptuous wedding feast, with entertainment by some boy actors (foreground), appear in the painting at right. It is from a colorful panorama of the life of an Elizabethan nobleman.

respected yeoman farmer who had died the year before. Anne lived with her family in Shottery, a tiny hamlet in the parish of Stratford only a mile or so across the fields from where the Shakespeares lived. A marriage license was issued to William and Anne at Worcester on November 27. The ceremony must have taken place soon afterward, but the actual date cannot be traced.

In Stratford at that time it was customary for the oldest son to bring his bride to live in his father's house. William Shakespeare probably did this, for John Shakespeare's property on Henley Street had space enough for another family. And a family it soon became. The young Shakespeares' first daughter, Susanna, was born in May, 1583. She was followed in January, 1585, by a twin brother and sister, Hamnet and Judith.

Although devoted to his family, Shakespeare had apparently become more and more enthralled with the players' craft and the art of the theatre. What had impressed him strongly as a child was irresistible to him as a young man. Because of a desire to work in the theatre, Shakespeare may have joined an acting company that played in Stratford. Or he may have followed a troupe of actors who had appeared there. His course was set; he decided to leave Stratford.

The date of his departure is unknown, but it seems plausible that within two years of the birth of his twins he left. And in all of England there was only one place where a restless young man with a hunger for excitement could go. That place was London.

25

BOTH: PHOTOS BY DEREK BAYES

THE STRATFORD COUNTRYSIDE

For three hundred years before Shakespeare's birth, the thinly populated English countryside was a pattern of forests, snug towns surrounded by large farms, and lonely mansions. Like landowners in other counties of England, yeomen of Warwickshire lived in half-timbered houses such as the two shown here. Between the heavy oak beams were walls of brick or of twigs and mud; roofs were generally of thatch that looked like layers of frosting spread over the gables and dormers. The best-known example of this picturesque building-type is Anne Hathaway's cottage (left). Another example is the comfortable farm in Wilmcote where Shakespeare's mother lived (above). At the time of Shakespeare's birth, the character of the countryside around Stratford began to change noticeably. Farms became generally smaller, and farmhouses were made of stone instead of timber—the forests were shrinking as the population swelled. Also, great houses appeared on prominent sites, built by courtiers willing to spend lavishly to entertain their Queen. A few castlelike manors had been erected in Warwickshire during the reigns of Elizabeth's predecessors (see overleaf). But those gloomy residences were now outnumbered and outshone by mansions in a new and foreign fashion. The countryside, which had slept through centuries of medieval isolation, was awakening to a new age.

27

*Compton Wynyates, a castlelike manor with battlemented
towers and twisted chimneys, was completed about 1520.*

*The long galleries of England's country houses were hung
with brilliant tapestries. This one shows a rural scene.*

*One of the early, splendid Elizabethan
houses was Charlecote, near Stratford.*

PHOTO BY DEREK BAYES

1408

Farmers, tradesmen, and players came
to Stratford over the stone arches of
Clopton Bridge, which spans the Avon.

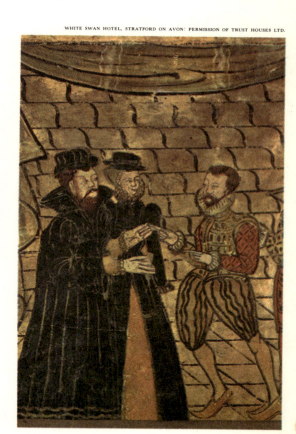

Painted on the wall of a hotel in Stratford is a scene of a
young Elizabethan man about to leave home for London.

PERMISSION OF THE TRUSTEES OF THE BRITISH MUSEUM

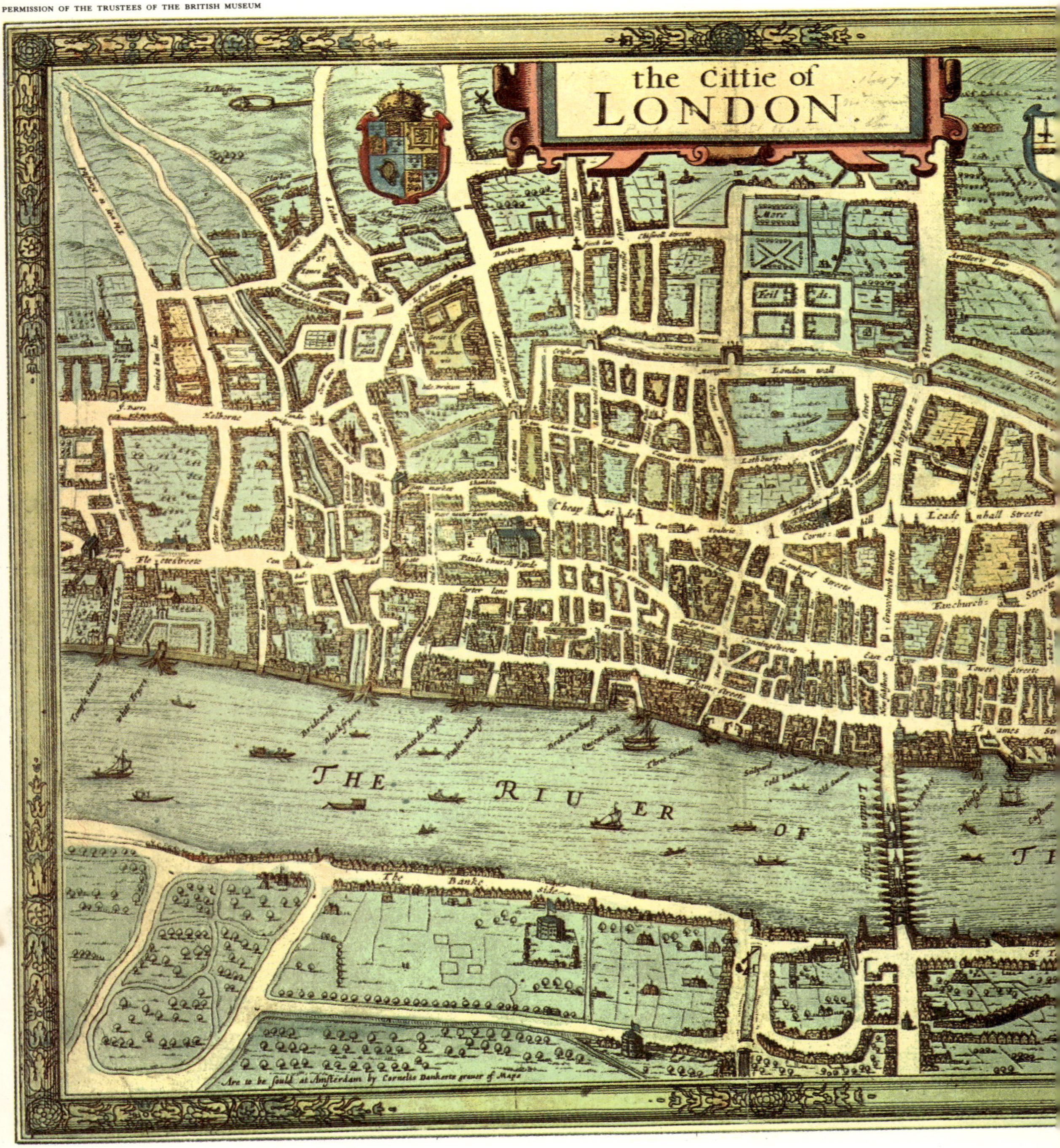

LONDON

II

Following the road from Stratford, Shakespeare must have entered London through Newgate, the western entrance to the walled city. From this vantage point he had his first view of the cluster of buildings that lay in the distance and formed the heart of the city. The streets leading into the center were largely residential, each lined with low wooden dwellings.

London, like Stratford, lay along a river. The Thames, that broad ribbon of pale blue water, formed London's southern boundary. Traffic on the river was constant; at almost any time or tide one could see barges crowded with passengers, great flatboats loaded with produce, and tall-masted merchantmen bound for foreign ports. Perhaps even the barge that belonged to Queen Elizabeth was there, tended by servants in royal livery.

Spanning the Thames was the sprawling length of London Bridge, jammed to overflowing with houses and shops. Customers heavy-laden with goods they had bought pushed their way over its jagged pavement. And peddlers, who were called chapmen, moved back and forth from shore to shore. It must have seemed to young Shakespeare that all the world had moved to this big city.

London was indeed noted for its crowds. And the population continued to increase as more and more people swarmed to the metropolis in search of opportunity. What they saw when they got there was described by one of Shakespeare's contemporaries, the playwright Thomas Dekker:

In every street, carts and coaches make such a thundering as if the world ran upon wheels. At every corner, men, women, and children meet in such shoals that posts are set up . . . to strengthen the houses, lest with jostling one another they should shoulder

In 1604, when this map of London was made, the city was bounded on the south by the Thames and on other sides by a wall. Across London Bridge was the entertainment district, an area called The Banke Side on the map.

them down. Besides, hammers are beating in one place, tubs hooping in another, pots clinking in a third, water tankards running at a tilt in a fourth. Here are porters sweating under burdens, there, merchants' men bearing bags of money. Chapmen (as if they were at leapfrog) skip out of one shop into another. Tradesmen . . . are lusty at legs and never stand still.

The London streets were muddy, narrow, and noisy, and they reeked of the slops that were spilled from second-story windows. The ground floors of many houses were shops where busy merchants made and sold their wares. There were goldsmiths, booksellers, apothecaries, and grocers. Apprentices, standing before their masters' doors, added to the noise and confusion by calling "What lack you, sir?" to people passing by. Over their cries and the clanking of cart wheels, the ballad mongers could be heard singing tunes from the song sheets they were peddling. And street criers, hawking foodstuffs from trays hung around their necks, shouted continually with coarse, raw voices.

By the time Shakespeare arrived, London was beginning to free itself from its medieval bonds. The city was expanding physically to accommodate the influx—literally pushing against its confining city walls. The Royal Exchange had recently been completed, the most important new building in the city. Also, three structures designed specifically for the acting of plays had just been constructed—the only ones of their kind in England.

A watchman pacing and a pauper begging were usual city sights.

The first playhouse, completed in 1576, was built by a prominent actor named James Burbage. To finance this undertaking, he had obtained money from his wife's brother, a prosperous grocer, after giving persuasive assurance that a theatre would be a good investment. Then Burbage had acquired some property just north of London, facing a large, undeveloped area called Finsbury Fields.

Since the site had formerly been owned by the Church, it was beyond the control of the London council—which was precisely why Burbage had chosen it. Attending plays was a merry pastime for many Londoners, including the nobility, but the Puritans deemed it a sinful activity. So did members of the city council—businessmen who tended to be wary of the acting profession. So many restrictions had been placed on actors in London that Burbage felt compelled to build his theatre outside the city's jurisdiction.

With money to build and with land to build on, Burbage lacked only a plan. Two ideas seem to have dominated his thinking as he considered the best possible design. The first idea was that England's improvised innyard theatres worked fairly well. At any rate, they offered a central area in front of the stage in which the lowest rank of customers could stand. These so-called groundlings, who paid only a penny, were nearly always rowdy and sometimes uncontrollable, but since they composed a substantial portion of the audience, their favor had to be sought. The stage was

The colorful spectacle of London as viewed from the Thames' south bank is displayed in this engraving made early in the seventeenth century. St. Paul's Cathedral is the tall, imposing structure in the panel at left. London Bridge, jammed tight with narrow buildings, is prominent in the panel above.

With his white silk hose, padded doublet, and thick lacy ruff, this elegant, curly-haired young man appears the perfect Elizabethan fop.

36

The round bull- and bear-baiting rings, located across the Thames from London, are seen in this detail from a sixteenth-century map.

set up at one end of the rectangular courtyard, and the inn's galleries, arranged in tiers, formed the remaining three sides. Here the higher-paying customers sat and watched in relative comfort.

The second idea that seemed useful to Burbage was the concept of the bull- and bear-baiting rings. These arenas stood on the south bank of the Thames. There, to the delight of Elizabethan sports enthusiasts, chained bears and bulls were attacked by mastiffs—clawed at and bitten until they were brought down and mauled. The great advantage of the rings' design was that it allowed more people to be near the center of action. Burbage decided his building should be roughly circular in order to give his customers the best chance to see and hear what occurred on the stage. And the rectangular stage itself should jut out into the area occupied by the groundlings.

Refining his design still further, he added a partial roof. It was simply a rim of thatch projecting from the outside of the structure, but it covered the seated patrons and the actors' rooms backstage. There was also a slanted roof over the stage itself and a peaked roof on the backstage tower. In case of sudden rain, only the groundlings stood the chance of getting wet, and they were used to it.

Burbage's playhouse, which may have accommodated about fifteen hundred persons, was called, simply, The Theatre. It was followed within a few years by other playhouses of similar design. The first of these, erected near The Theatre, was called the Curtain—after the Curtain family, who had once owned the land it stood on. The other structure, the Rose, was built on the south bank of the Thames, near the bear-baiting ring.

Although scenery was not used in these theatres, each was equipped with elaborate facilities to assist the staging of plays. In designing The Theatre, Burbage had allowed for five different levels on which his actors could work. At the bottom were trap doors built into the floor of the stage. When these doors were open, an actor, standing on a platform below stage level, could play a scene like the graveside episode Shakespeare later wrote for *Hamlet*. The platform could also be drawn up to stage level. On it a devil or a ghost could crouch, and then as the platform rose, leap forth in a burst of fireworks or a puff of smoke to smite the senses of the audience.

The second level was the stage itself, where most of the action took place. Behind it was a shallow enclosure that was nearly always the setting for an interior scene. The main stage could be a great hall, a battlefield, or even a busy street; the enclosure might be the inside of a shop, for example, or part of a throne room.

One level above the main stage was the balcony, which could serve as anything from a mountaintop to a battlement. If a play required that a town be assaulted, the besiegers would appear on the main stage and the defenders would be seen on the balcony, as though on the summit of city walls. Behind the balcony, on the same level, was the "tiring room" where the actors attired themselves in their costumes. Directly above, on the fourth level, were the storage lofts where props and costumes were kept. Between these two rooms was a musicians' gallery. Here they blew their trumpets to signal the start of battle scenes. But the musicians were not always confined to this gallery. Often they were part of the action on stage—particularly during coronations—and they were even known to play their instruments in the space beneath the main stage.

At the top level of the theatre, just under the roof of the tower, were pulleys and other bits of concealed machinery. Using these devices, the prop man could send stuffed birds or the images of goddesses—even thunderbolts—down to the stage. Despite its limitations, Burbage's design provided for a multitude of dazzling stage effects.

James Burbage's playhouse, with its curved galleries and extended platform stage, combined the best elements of an Elizabethan inn and a bear-baiting ring. The Swan (at right) was a later adaptation of the Burbage design.

tectum

porticus

sedilia

orchestra

ingressus

mimorum
ædes

proscænium·

planities siue arena.

quintum sed dispari et structura, bestiarum concitati
oni destinatum, in quo multi ursi, tauri, et stupenda
magnitudinis canes, distinctis cautis et septis aluntur; qui
ad

A tiltyard, where jousters dueled in armor, is shown here in an odd perspective. In Elizabethan times, men jousted more for sport than for honor.

Elizabethans liked to watch tennis being played; it was, however, a rich man's sport. The hand-strung rackets were expensive, as were the fragile tennis balls—made of leather shells stuffed with hair.

In the 1580's the English theatre flourished, even as Puritan preachers warned that the souls of all those who entered the playhouses would be corrupted. Young apprentices, to whom a penny meant a great deal, flocked to see plays. They lined up many hours in advance of a performance, hoping they could find a spot that would offer a good view of the stage. Women too were avid playgoers; they went often, and at times without male escorts.

Queen Elizabeth herself was an enthusiastic spectator at theatrical performances given at court. She also enjoyed many of the other amusements and sports in which her subjects participated: fairs, tennis matches, morris dancing, hunting, and jousting. The Crown licensed the bowling alleys, and occasionally bear-baiting matches were staged as official entertainments for distinguished foreign visitors.

The Queen, though intense and intellectual, had a lively wit and a certain theatrical flair. She enjoyed the adulation of her subjects and encouraged it by frequent displays of showmanship. She could often be seen in the streets of London, transported in a caravan so ornate as to suggest one of the pageants that had been adorned for a mystery play of old. And when she opened Parliament each year, she was carried through London in a gilded litter as twenty-four maids of honor in glittering costumes rode solemnly behind her.

Elizabeth looked forward each year to the appearance at court of one of the country's leading acting companies. Before the court performance, which generally took place at Christmastime, Elizabeth's Master of the Revels arranged to have many plays from the repertories of several companies acted for him. From these he selected the plays that would be most suitable for the Queen.

Often, these were plays that had been well tested on the popular stage. To compete with its rivals, each acting company in London presented a number of different plays every week, and only the best survived. New plays were generally put on as special attractions in the middle of the week, for there was usually a full house on weekends and holidays. Because audiences were eager for variety, it was not unheard of for one of these repertory companies to stage fifteen different plays during one month.

The members of an acting company were divided into three separate groups. The first was composed of senior

A laurel wreath afloat above him, the poet George Gascoigne offers a manuscript to Elizabeth in this fanciful pen-and-ink drawing. The poet's heroic appearance is aided by the lance and sword he bears, but as a badge of his craft he has a pen tucked behind his ear. High above him, through an elliptical opening in the ceiling, a godlike arm protrudes. Suspended from it is a Latin motto that can be loosely translated to read, "As much by war as by eloquence."

actors, the more experienced members of the company. These men were sometimes called sharers because they held stock in the company and thus shared in its profits. The second group comprised the hired men, who were paid a weekly wage and did not hold a share. They performed a number of backstage jobs in the theatre, and all but the prompter were capable actors. Hired men played the minor roles, and they played more than one role in a production. Under the rigors of the repertory system, the hired men might have appeared in as many as fifty plays a year. And if one of them had writing talent, he might be called on now and then to rework a speech for an important senior actor.

Boy actors made up the third group. They played children's roles in all the plays. And since women were not permitted on the stage during the reign of Elizabeth— or for several decades thereafter—boys with unchanged voices also played the female roles. Boy actors had to be extremely talented to play these parts convincingly, and they were, of course, well trained. Even so, a playwright had to approach his task with the idea that dialogue rather than physical action would best express most feminine emotions. As Shakespeare later proved in his *Antony and Cleopatra*, a great and passionate love affair could be suggested through brilliantly written conversation. In most plays, however, the women's roles were smaller and less important than the men's.

Many boys continued to work in the theatre during their adolescence and grew up to be respected senior actors. The competition for membership in good companies was keen, so a former boy-actor who brought years of experience to his work had a marked advantage over the come-lately performer—like Shakespeare—who entered the profession in his twenties.

It is not known how Shakespeare became part of the acting profession after arriving in London. Some Shakespearean scholars think he first worked in the company that was under the patronage of the Earl of Pembroke. Whether it was Pembroke's Men or some other company, Shakespeare would have been a junior member—a hired man— and as such would have had to work hard and practice continually.

The skills demanded of Elizabethan actors were many. Battles and sieges were popular with audiences, as were duels and murders. An actor had to know how to carry on hand-to-hand combat and how to take violent falls without

A performer had to be so skillful that he could effectively play the part of a woman (below) as well as portray a nobleman defending himself with dagger and rapier (above).

injuring himself or tearing his costume. And he had to be a superlative swordsman—so proficient that he could convince the audience that he was dueling to the death and not merely trading thrusts with another actor. He also had to be agile and light-footed, with a good sense of rhythm. Many plays had scenes in which the actors had to dance, and some plays were concluded with a dance performed by several members of the company.

An actor had to be articulate and have a rich, expressive voice. He was expected to bring out the poetry in a playwright's lines as well as create a plausible characterization. And he had to be heard over the hubbub of the groundlings, who, during the less dramatic parts of a play, often ate and drank and chattered among themselves. His voice had to have variety too, for all but the leading actors played more than one part in a production.

Acting different roles every afternoon meant that an actor's memory was as important as his voice. He had to know his lines perfectly; he could not expect a fellow actor to come to his rescue if he suffered a sudden lapse of memory while on stage. He could not even depend on the prompter, for this man was always bustling about, trying to get actors on and off the stage at the right time, making sure all the props were available, and testing to see that the visual effects worked properly.

Shakespeare may have possessed some acting potential when he left his home in Stratford, but he had a lot to learn. The more experienced members of a company were responsible for teaching the boys and the hired men the skills of their craft: fencing, dancing, and projecting their voices. Yet the ability to make dramatic characters come to life on the stage, as well as the ability to create them in writing, could not be learned. These gifts grew only from talent.

Shakespeare may not have come to London with a desire to write. But he arrived in the city at a time when writers were in demand, and the opportunities for a talented young man were plain to see. Acting companies were hard pressed to find new plays that would attract and hold London audiences.

Playwriting was a relatively new craft then, for the professional theatre had only begun to assert its influence on English literature. Prior to the 1500's there had been neither the cash nor a reason to pay writers—all the plays had been produced free of charge by amateurs, and the spoken parts were simply adapted from late medieval dramas. But as the players' companies prospered, the need for fresh material increased, and playwrights were suddenly in business.

From the start there were two distinct—and mutually hostile—groups of writers for the stage. One consisted of students and recent university graduates whose works were often more literary than dramatic. The other comprised various actors and clerks, and anyone else with a facile pen but little education. The works of the latter group lacked grace and polish but had the raw humor and pell-mell action that so delighted Elizabethan audiences.

In selling his work, a writer surrendered all control over it. His play became the property of an acting company. Once performed, however, it could easily be pirated by a publisher or by an actor from a rival company. A man needed only attend the theatre, jot down or memorize the dialogue he heard, and the play was his. Many plays found

Surrounded by fallen comrades and attacking enemies, the evil monarch in Richard III *awaits death. Shakespeare adapted this play, and others he wrote about England's kings, from the stories in Holinshed's* Chronicles.

45

The Tragicall History
of the Life and Death
of Doctor FAVSTVS.

With new Additions.

Written by *Ch. Mar.*

Printed at London for *John Wright*, and are to be sold at his
shop without Newgate, 1624.

Above is the title page of Doctor Faustus, *the play that Marlowe wrote around 1588. It shows the clever doctor making his contract with the Devil.*

their way into print by this means. But very often what was printed was a jumbled, corrupt version of the original: the result of bad copying or an actor's poor memory.

Pirated plays, appearing in hastily and badly printed editions, were sold by various booksellers in London, but no matter how many copies were purchased, the playwright was not a single penny richer. When he sold his play, it could be published and resold, and even shortened, without his consent. Material written for the stage was perishable indeed; though this must have angered many playwrights, it did not diminish their efforts.

One of the most important playwrights of this time was Christopher Marlowe. Although Marlowe had been university trained, he had adapted his literary talents to the taste of the Elizabethan audience without forfeiting his status among the university intellectuals. Marlowe's writing was full of excitement and passion, and it had a beauty of language that English playwrights before him had been unable to achieve. With Marlowe came an appreciation of eloquence, for he was a poet, the first of his kind to write for the English theatre.

The Earl of Pembroke's company was fortunate to have Marlowe in its service. If Shakespeare was indeed a member of this company, he would have had the example of that extraordinarily gifted man to guide him. The guidance could not have been long lasting, however, for Marlowe was killed in a tavern brawl in 1593. He was twenty-nine, Shakespeare's age. In the brief, brilliant span of his career he had written works that were both popular hits and literary triumphs. If Shakespeare was to be more than a patchwork artist who reworked other men's plays, he too would have to succeed as a literary and popular writer.

Another leading playwright of the 1580's was Robert Greene, who boasted that his talents had been developed at both Oxford and Cambridge. Greene despised all actors, and his ire extended to actor-authors like Shakespeare. He hated them because members of the acting companies profited greatly from successful play production, whereas the writers received little reward. He hated them also because he and his associates feared that literary standards were being lowered by the success of the unacademic writers.

In the summer of 1592, Greene developed a fatal illness. Although death was slow to come, he knew his life was ebbing away. He wrote furiously during his decline— venting his spleen in a series of pamphlets. Greene's bitter-

In this gallery of playwrights are Christopher Marlowe (bottom), a shrouded Robert Greene (top), and Thomas Nashe in chains—a woodcut from a book that maligns him.

The page reproduced above is from the pamphlet by Robert Greene in which he alludes to Shakespeare.

ness was directed against actors—on whom he blamed his ultimate poverty. In his last pamphlet, he addressed some remarks to three other intellectual playwrights. One of them is assumed to have been Marlowe. Greene implored his cohorts to stop writing plays for the actors by whom they had been exploited, "for it is a pity men of such rare wits should be subject to the pleasure of such rude grooms." He entreated them to take heed from his misery, and concluded his remarks by saying:

Yes, trust them not. For there is an upstart crow, beautified with our feathers, that with his tiger's heart wrapped in a player's hide supposes he is well able to bombast out a blank verse as the best of you. And being an absolute *Johannes fac totum* [Jack-of-all-trades] is in his own conceit the only Shake-scene in a country. O, that I might entreat your rare wits to be employed in the more profitable courses, and let those apes imitate your past excellence and never more acquaint them with your admired inventions.

This pamphlet, titled *Greene's Groatsworth of Wit*, was licensed for publication about two weeks after Greene's death. His words made it abundantly clear that the university writers were being challenged by a young man who was an actor as well as a playwright—and who, incidentally, was not a product of Cambridge or Oxford. If there was any doubt as to the identity of "Shake-scene," it could be pointed out that Greene's reference to a "tiger's heart wrapped in a player's hide" was a parody of a line from Shakespeare's *Henry VI*: "O tiger's heart wrapp'd in a woman's hide!" Greene's pamphlet thus contained the first documentary reference to Shakespeare in London. It is apparent that by 1592 the newcomer from Stratford was well established as both a playwright and an actor.

Henry VI was the first of Shakespeare's works about English kings (the so-called history plays). It had been written in three parts, but not consecutively. There is reason to believe that part one appeared some time after parts two and three. Although the play as a whole lacked the brilliance of such later works as *Henry V* and *Richard II*, it was an impressive piece of craftsmanship and one to which an apprentice playwright might proudly affix his name. The play profited by its strong appeal to patriotism. The English defeat at Orléans in 1429 was attributed solely to the sorcery of Joan of Arc, and the battle itself was staged with great theatrical force. English soldier players scaled ladders to duel with the French defenders of Orléans, who fought stubbornly from the balcony over the stage.

The playhouse literally vibrated with the dramatic excitement.

Shakespeare had demonstrated that, like Marlowe, he could combine literary merit with vigorous action. And to this fortunate combination he brought a rare knowledge of stagecraft. His star ascended, but his rise to fame as a playwright was interrupted. Late in 1592, London was struck by an epidemic that threatened the life of every resident: the bubonic plague. Until this danger had passed, every human effort would be directed toward survival.

Whenever they became writers, men of position hoped for royal patronage. This picture of Sir William Teshe, with his inscription to the "noble Quene," appears in the elegant volume he presented to her.

49

THE QUEEN AND HER COURT

The best show in London when William Shakespeare arrived in 1587 was Queen Elizabeth and her court. With five hundred gowns as rich as the high-shouldered, pearl-studded dress at right, she dazzled the noblemen and adventurers who surrounded her, and brought them to their knees. And by making herself the target of all eyes in the very streets of London, as well as in her palaces, she changed the unpopular monarchy into a powerful and respected instrument of government. She was as thrifty as she was vain, preferring to be entertained in her noblemen's homes and to receive gifts rather than to buy and spend. She was also ruthless and changeable. Although Sir Wal-

ter Raleigh had been her favorite for ten years and had named the richest part of a new continent after her ("Virginia" alluded to her unmarried state), she sent him off to the Tower when he had the audacity to marry one of her maids in waiting. She later pardoned him. He appears below at the height of his career, wearing the paunchy doublet of the day, one earring, and a fur-collared cape over his shoulder. The Elizabethan court set brilliant new styles and fostered the arts, but it also had a historic mission: to build a stable and united England. As one courtier said: "The Queen did fish for men's souls, and had so sweet a bait that no one could escape her network."

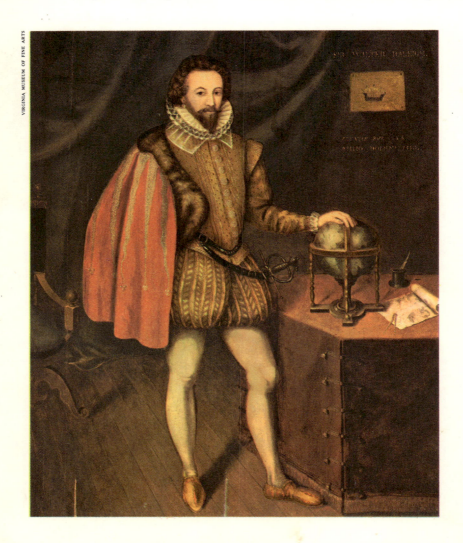

Elizabeth was sixty-seven when this scene of Lord and Lady Russell's wedding procession was painted in 1600

Yet she looks as youthful as the bride (in white at far right), and more powerful than the courtiers who carry her.

*Elizabeth visited Longleat House on a royal progress. In an age of splendid houses,
it was notable for its classical symmetry, large windows, and Italian-style luxury.*

A regal party is seen above leaving Whitehall Palace in the royal barge.

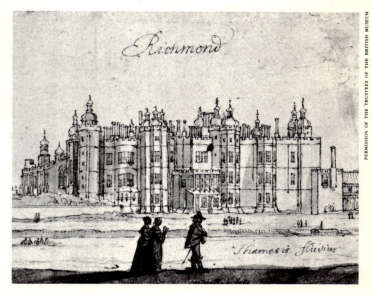

As viewed from the water, Richmond Palace was a mass of chimneys and spires.

55

PLAYERS ON TOUR

"The cause of plagues is sin, if you look to it well; and the cause of sin are plays; therefore the cause of plagues are plays." This declaration by a London preacher summed up the feelings of many people that the sins of the city had invited the ugly punishment brought by the plague.

If sinful drama was the cause, it was promptly remedied. When the plague reached epidemic proportions in the late summer of 1592, people were prohibited from attending all public meeting places for reasons of health, and the London theatres were closed along with everything else. Soon, according to one eyewitness, ". . . playhouses [were standing] like taverns that have cast out their masters, the doors locked up, the flags . . . taken down—or rather like houses lately infected, from whence the affrighted dwellers are fled."

The theatres having closed, the actors immediately began making plans to go on tour. Many acting companies combined forces, merging the talents of two or more to ease the financial and physical burdens of touring. Other companies tried to make ends meet by selling their stock of plays to printers. More plays were published during the plague years than in any previous years. Printers were not very discriminating; many of the plays that received publication were of such inferior quality that they would otherwise have vanished forever.

The plague that struck London in 1592 was no new terror. It had scourged England periodically for a hundred years. In the Middle Ages it had been known in Europe as the Black Death because the bodies of its victims turned black.

With its crazing fever and racking pain, plague crept in from the wharves and river mouths where goods from foreign ports were unloaded. Rats haunting the ships carried the fleas that spread the infection. But the Elizabeth-

Carrying props as well as torches to light their way, a troupe of traveling players form an elegant caravan in this German water color of the late sixteenth century. The actors are dressed in the costumes they wear on stage.

ans did not know this. They killed stray dogs, which they thought were disease carriers, and let the fleas continue working their evil.

None of the commonly used medical remedies made of herbs and spices had any effect, so a number of folk cures were attempted. In one of these, live chickens were applied to the patient's swollen flesh in an effort to draw out the disease. One chicken after another was applied like a poultice until each one died. If a chicken did not die, it was assumed—erroneously—that the patient had been purged of the plague. There were few recoveries, however.

Ten per cent of the London populace died in the plague of 1592. It seemed as if the city itself were dying. Plague victims were disposed of immediately, the bodies carried directly to a specially designated burial place. Only the privileged and the wealthy had the luxury of a church service.

The wealthy and highborn were best equipped to escape the disease, for most of them had country homes away from afflicted areas of London. The hope that the clean air of the hinterlands would save their lives drove many of these frightened people out of London in coaches hung with supposedly purifying herbs. Others who fled the city

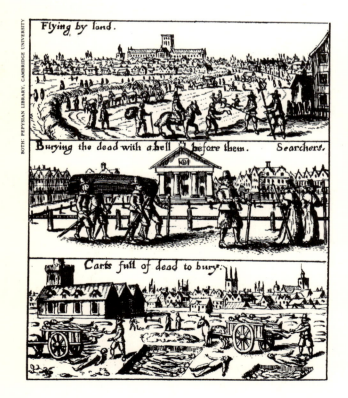

Flea-bearing rats spread bubonic plague through London, creating scenes like those at left. A rat catcher on his rounds appears in the woodcut above, an illustration from a ballad. At right is a portion of a pamphlet that listed all of London's plague fatalities and implored divine help for the city.

LORD HAVE MERCY UPON US.

This is the humble Petition of *England* unto Almighty God, meekely imploring his Divine bounty for the cessation of this Mortality of Pestilence now raigning amongst us: VVith a lamentable List of Deaths Triumphs in the weekly Burials of the City of LONDON, and the Parishes adjacent to the same.

LORD SHew thy pity on this sinfull Land,
Have We not felt enough thy heavy hand:
Mercy We beg of thee, doe not sweete God
Vpon Thy people too long lay thy Rod;
Vs In thine anger doe not quite consume,
LORD Let our prayers ascend like sweete perfume:
Have Thou regard unto our moane, and showe
Mercy On them that prostrate lye below
Vpon The ground; O doe not strictly call
Vs To account, for we have sinned all.
LORD Be propitious, spare, O spare though wee
Have Been rebellious children unto thee:
Mercy Is still in store for those who will
Vpon Amendment leave their former ill.
Vs Wretched sinners unto grace receive,
LORD We have sinned, now our sins wee'll leave:
Have Thou commiseration on our griefe,
Mercy We want, relying (for reliefe)
Vpon Thy wonted favours; for thou hast
Vs Pardon'd often for offences past.
LORD Let us finde, for we doe humbly seeke,
Have Thou compassion, now our mindes are meeke
Mercy May enter: Thou imprint'st thy grace
Vpon Those hearts where pride can have no place.
Vs Then admit into thy favour for,
LORD Our iniquities we doe abhor:
Have We so wicked been, that thou canst not
Mercy Afford? O is thy wrath so hot
Vpon Us that it can't be quencht with teares?
Vs Thou hast spar'd (indeed) for many yeares.
LORD We confesse it, yet on our repentance,
Have Pitty and revoke thy dreadfull sentence:
Mercy O mercy still we crave, we cry,
Vpon Us Lord have mercy, or we dye.
Vs Thou hast plagued with the Pestilence,
LORD Stay thy hand upon our penitence:
Have Minde (good God) that we are dust and clay,
Mercy From thee we want, for this we pray;
Vpon Our wretched states look favourable,
Vs In thine ire rebuke not, we're unable
LORD To doe any good without thy ayde:
Have Pitty then, let these petitions made,
Mercy Invoke from thy supernall throne,
Vpon Our misery be thy favour showne,
Vs In our wants relieve, let us not cry
LORD Unto thee in vaine for remedy;
Have We not cause to weepe, and with our cryes
Mercy To aske; O let thy gentle eyes
Vpon Our miseries reflect; O heale
Vs Both in soule and body; we appeale
Unto thy mercy; Sicknesse hath undone us,
What can we say, but, *Lord have mercy upon us.*

Amen Say I, *M. P.*

A Prayer fit be used in this time of sicknesse or mortality.

O *Lord most just, and Father most mercifull, thou it is that renewest thy Plagues against Man when he offendeth thee: thy vengeance from heaven is both sudden and fearefull toward the rebellious and disobedient children: thou for one sin in King* David, *destroyedst with the loathsome disease of the Pestilence many thousands of his people: cast thine eyes of mercy upon us, O thou preserver of men, which languish now in this land, and in this house with the like disease and sicknesse. Now, deare God, hath not* David *onely offended thee, in trusting to his strength, and numbring of his people: but even each congregation; and every houshold hath one way or other provoked thee to plague thy disobedient people: and now that we see thy plagues appearing, to the piercing and parting of our bodies and soules asunder: Lord, we stand amazed in our mindes, heartily sighing with groanes at sight of our sins. Now we consider, we have sinned grievously, we have done amisse, we have dealt wickedly, we have lived ungodly, wee have swerved from the way of truth, without any godly feare or remorse of conscience: thy great benefit of Peace, and rare blessing of long prosperity, under so good and gracious a Governor, have brought too too many of us, to such security and contempt of Religion, that altogether forgetting to be thankfull, we have abused thy benefits as fast as they came, and that with a churlish kinde of impiety: the thoughts of our hearts, the words of our mouthes, and the works of our hands are vain, carnall, and devillish: yea, our service to thee oftentimes but meere abomination: so farre (alas) have we erred from the path of thy commandements. As thou didst finde with the Israelites wickednes in* Gilgal, *sin in* Bethel, *and iniquity in* Bersheba; *so in every Church, in every Court, nay, in every concourse or assembly amongst us, thou beholdest how the flesh hath overgrown the Spirit, and how reason is over-ruled with affections: so many labour in these our dayes under the displayed ensigne of satan, that very few (deare Father) are found setled in the dutifull form of upright and spirituall obedience, which thou requirest. We confesse, thou mightest justly therefore forsake us, as we have forsaken thee: and not onely proceed to sting the head-Cities, and whole body of this land, with sundry plagues and grievous diseases; but for our manifold sins and iniquities, which we daily commit, thou mightst justly and worthily condemne us, man after man, to eternall death, all consciences being so guilty, that they already condemne themselves. Yet who is he (O mercifull Lord) that can measure thy goodnesse, who by thy word doest oftentimes bring sinners to beliefe, repentance, and salvation? though it be not thy pleasure (good Lord) to make the wicked innocent, but rather to visit their iniquities, yet have we this comfort, that thy mercy to the humble ever rests unmeasurable and unmoveable: though thou speakest to the Prophet against thine own people, being disobedient to thee, saying,* Though Moses and Samuel stood before me, yet have I no heart to this people: Drive them away that they may go out of my sight, some unto death, some to the sword, and some to captivity: *yet we know (O our good God) that when as* Ephraim *was heard lamenting and praying heartily in this distresse, thou thoughtest then upon mercy, as a Father pittying his own children. This thy clemency to others incourageth us to cry for thy mercies, in this our misery, upon our repentance, both for us, ours, and the whole land. Be intreated therefore to pitty this land, and the infected people thereof, that we may all say, The Lord liveth for ever, worthy of praise, because he hath been mercifull unto sinners.* Amen.

Printed at London for *Thomas Lambert* at the signe of the Horse-shoo in Smithfield.

An exact and true relation of the number of those that were buried in London and the Liberties of all diseases, from the 17. of March 1592. to 22. of December, 1593.

		totall.	Pl.
March	17	351	31
March	24	219	29
March	31	307	27
April	7	203	33
April	14	290	37
April	21	310	41
April	28	350	29
May	5	339	38
May	12	300	42
May	19	450	58
May	26	410	62
Iune	2	441	81
Iune	9	399	99
Iune	16	401	108
Iune	23	850	118
Iune	30	1440	927
Iuly	7	1510	893
Iuly	14	1491	958
Iuly	21	1507	852
Iuly	28	1503	983
August	4	1550	797
August	11	1532	651
August	18	1508	449
August	25	1490	507
Septemb.	1	1210	563
Septemb	8	621	451
Septem.	15	629	349
Septem	22	450	130
Septem	29	408	327
Octob.	6	422	323
Octob.	13	310	328
Octob.	20	320	302
Octob.	27	310	301
Novem.	3	309	209
Nov.	10	301	107
Nov.	17	321	93
Nov.	24	349	94
Decemb.	1	331	86
Decemb	8	329	71
Decem	15	386	39
Decem.	22		

Baptized. 5817.
The totall. 25886.
Of the Plague. 11503.

1603.
Buried in London & the Liberties, of all Diseases, Anno 1603. the number here following.

		totall.	Pl.
March	17	108	3
March	24	60	2
March	31	78	6
April	7	66	4
April	14	79	4
April	21	98	[illegible]
April	28	109	10
May	5	90	11
May	12	112	18
May	19	122	22
May	26	122	32
Iune	2	114	30
Iune	9	131	43
Iune	16	144	59
Iune	23	182	72
Iune	30	267	158
Iuly	7	445	263
Iuly	14	612	424

The Out-parishes this Weeke were joyned with the City.

Iuly	21	1186	917
Iuly	28	1728	1392
August	4	2256	1925
August	11	2077	1743
August	18	3054	2719
August	25	2853	2535
Septemb.	1	3385	3034
Septemb.	8	3078	2728
Septem	15	3129	2815
Septem.	22	2456	2192
Septem.	29	1961	1731
Octob.	6	1831	1649
Octob.	13	1312	1142
Octob.	20	766	648
Octob.	27	615	504
Novem.	3	737	592
Nov.	10	585	441
Nov.	17	384	255
Nov.	24	198	102
Decem.	1	223	105
Decem.	8	163	55
Decem	15	200	66
Decem.	22	168	74

The totall of the Burials this whole Yeare, 38250.
Of the Plague, 30583.

1625.

		totall.	Pl.
March	17	262	4
March	24	226	8
March	31	243	11
April	7	239	10
April	14	256	24
April	21	230	25
April	28	305	26
May	5	292	30
May	12	332	45
May	19	379	71
May	26	401	78
Iune	2	395	69
Iune	9	434	91
Iune	16	510	165
Iune	23	640	239
Iune	30	942	390
Iuly	7	1222	593
Iuly	14	1781	1004
Iuly	21	2850	1819
Iuly	28	3583	2471
August	4	4517	3659
August	11	4855	4115
August	18	5205	4463
August	25	4841	4218
Septemb.	1	3897	3344
Septemb.	8	3157	2550
Septem.	15	2148	1672
Septem	22	1994	1551
Septem.	29	1236	852
Octob.	6	833	538
Octob.	13	815	511
Octob.	20	651	331
Octob.	27	375	134
Novem.	3	357	89
Nov.	10	319	92
Nov.	17	274	48
Nov.	24	231	27
Decem.	1	293	15
Decem.	8	181	15
Decem.	15	168	6
Decem.	22	157	1

The totall of the Burials this whole yeare, 54082.
Of the Plague. 35428.

1630.
The true number of all that dyed of severall diseases, Anno 1630. at the lower end truly calculated and summed up, though here beginning as followeth.

		totall.	Pl.
Iune	24	205	19
Iuly	1	209	25
Iuly	8	217	43
Iuly	15	250	50
Iuly	22	229	40
Iuly	29	279	77
August	5	250	56
August	12	246	65
August	19	269	54
August	26	270	67
Septemb.	2	230	66
Septemb.	9	259	63
Septem.	16	264	68
Septem	23	274	57
Septem.	30	269	56
Octob.	7	236	66
Octob.	14	261	73
Octob.	21	248	80
Octob.	28	214	34
Novem.	4	242	29
Nov.	11	215	29
Nov.	18	200	18
Nov.	25	226	7
Decemb.	2	221	20
Decemb.	9	198	19
Decem.	16	212	7

The totall of all the burials this yeare, is of all diseases. 10554.
Of the Plague. 1317.

1636.
Buried in London & the Liberties, of all diseases, the number as followeth.

		totall.	Pl.
April	7	199	2
April	14	205	4

This weeke was added to the City Parishes,
S. Marg. Westminster.
Lambeth.
S. Mary Newington.
Redriffe Parish.
S. Mary Islington.
Stepney Parish.
Hackney Parish.

April	21	285	14
April	28	259	17
May	5	215	10
May	12	308	55
May	19	299	35
May	26	330	62
Iune	2	339	67
Iune	9	345	87
Iune	16	381	103
Iune	23	304	79
Iune	30	352	104
Iuly	7	215	81
Iuly	14	372	104
Iuly	21	395	120
Iuly	28	423	151
August	4	461	206
August	11	538	283
August	18	638	321
August	25	787	429
Septem.	1	1011	638
Septem.	8	1069	650
Septem.	15	1306	865
Septem.	22	1229	775
Septem.	29	1403	928
Octob.	6	1405	921
Octob.	13	[illegible]	[illegible]
Octob.	20	[illegible]	[illegible]
Octob.	27		
Novem.	3		
Nov.	10		
Nov.	17		
Nov.	24		
Decemb.	1		
Decemb.	8		
Decem.	15		
Decem.	22		

The Queen sits erect in her glittering coach in this illustration called "Elizabeth and Fame" from William Teshe's book. The scene is imaginary. The coach's knobbed wheels would have created a bone-shaking ride for the Queen as well as for Fame ("fama"), the winged creature sounding a horn.

did so less elegantly. "Away they trudge," wrote Thomas Dekker, "thick and threefold, some riding, some on foot, some without boots, some in their slippers." On their way they must have seen the rotting bodies of those who had been cast out to die. Dekker stated: "In fields, in ditches . . . and under stalls, being either thrust by cruel masters out of doors or wanting all worldly succor but the common benefit of earth and air, [they] have most miserably perished."

Although the threat of plague was fearful and constant, it did not halt the pleasures of the aristocracy or the activities of the royal court, whose members were dispersed about the country. The Queen had wished to remain in London near her subjects, but she had been restrained from doing so by her advisers and sent off to the safety of the country.

Under normal circumstances the Queen spent her summers in the country, and there were houses in various parts of the kingdom to which she might go. They stood empty, awaiting her visit—at which time her furnishings would be brought in and the larders stocked with food. She visited other houses too, the estates of her noblemen and courtiers, who were prepared to entertain her lavishly for as long as she would stay.

Followed by an enormous troupe of servitors, and perhaps three hundred baggage carts, her magnificent coach would proceed slowly through the countryside. In the course of these royal progresses from one great house to another, the Queen would stop briefly in each of the provincial cities and towns along the way. Elizabeth recognized the importance of letting her subjects see her in all her regal splendor, and they in turn looked forward to her appearances. They lined the streets for hours waiting for her to pass. The sight of her strengthened their loyalty and drew them closer to her. She remained an alert politician, aware of her power to lift her people's sagging morale. Thus even at the time of the plague, when the mood of England was sorrowful, the Queen's progresses were no less splendid than before.

William Shakespeare may have returned to Stratford at times during the plague years, but he did not forsake London. Although theatres were closed and there was no outlet for new plays, his flow of writing continued uninterrupted. While the ban on public performances was in effect, Shakespeare was composing his first nondramatic work, a narrative poem called *Venus and Adonis*. Its ornate beauty soon brought him to the attention of aristocratic young

Londoners whose tastes favored elegant and refined verse.

It was a custom in Elizabethan times for a poet to present his work to a nobleman. In return, it was hoped that the man of rank would offer a handsome prize and perhaps even agree to become the poet's permanent patron. Shakespeare chose to honor the youthful Earl of Southampton, heir to a sizable fortune and ward of the Queen. In Nicholas Rowe's biography of Shakespeare, it is recorded that the Earl was so delighted by the poem that Shakespeare was rewarded for his effort with a sum of money large enough to sustain him awhile, if he wished to go on writing poetry.

Venus and Adonis was entered in the Stationers' Register on April 18, 1593. By then Shakespeare had also composed other works, including his first comic plays. Although his comedy *Love's Labour's Lost* is believed to have been written later, there is a legend that this was the play that the Earl of Pembroke's Men presented before the Queen at her country palace of Hampton Court during the Christmas season of 1592. (Court performances were neither hindered by the plague nor the shuttering of London's playhouses.) The style of *Love's Labour's Lost* suggests that Shakespeare must have had the court audience in mind when he wrote it. The dialogue of the play captures the fashionable wit and sophistication that were part of court manners, and which the groundlings at the theatres would not have liked.

Hampton Court, where the Queen spent Christmas in 1592, is now regarded as England's most beautiful royal residence. It lies near a bend in the river Thames fifteen miles southwest of London. The palace is essentially a brick structure composed of many courtyards and towers gracefully topped by pointed domes. In the sixteenth century, gold and silver were the dominant motifs of the interior. Tapestries sparkling with gold and silver thread adorned the walls, and the ceilings were thickly ornamented with gilded swirls.

Hampton Court was presented to Elizabeth's father, King Henry VIII, in 1526, and it soon became one of his favorite residences. He rebuilt much of it, constructed new royal apartments, and added a great hall in which plays were performed after Elizabeth took over the palace.

Performing at court had always been an honor for the

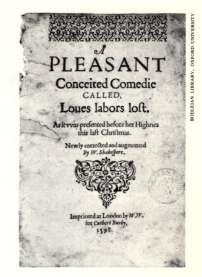

After finishing the comedy Love's Labour's Lost, *Shakespeare began a lyric poem that he dedicated to the Earl of Southampton (below).*

Though once dismissed as "a quantity of towers, turrets, and other baubles," Hampton Court has the splendor and symmetry of the best English palaces.

acting companies. It was also a strenuous chore, for it involved exhaustive preparations and many extra rehearsals. In the halls of a palace, the staging of plays was different from that in the London theatres. When at court, the players worked on a special stage built at one end of a high-ceilinged, rectangular room. Torches and candles—some hung from wires extending from one wall to another—produced the illumination normally provided by the afternoon sun. Great care was taken to make the costumes as elegant as time and money allowed; each was generously fashioned from such rich fabrics as taffeta, velvet, and cloth of gold. And to add to the indoor splendor, there were elaborate sets painted in meticulous detail to give the illusion of depth.

Flemish villagers attend an outdoor play in this painting by Jan Brueghel the Elder. The stage is set against an inn. The flag is raised to announce a performance.

Queen Elizabeth attends a lavishly outfitted court performance in this nineteenth-century engraving. The stage, set up in a palace hall, is graced with her own royal crest.

The theatre season at Elizabeth's court brought forth capacity audiences of elegant courtiers. All chattered freely until the Queen made her entrance, a few moments before the performance started. She was bejeweled and erect. Her face was powdered with a thick white mask that nearly obscured her wrinkles, and her costume was strangely bold for a woman no longer young. Her wig, a vivid red, matched the brilliance of her attire. In that hushed room, her strength was more impressive than her beauty.

Elizabeth knew a great deal about the theatre, and her standards were high. On at least one occasion, she had been known to call out to the actors on stage to speak louder. And when they did not speak up to her complete satisfaction, she moved her chair nearer the edge of its dais in the hope of hearing them better.

Actors had to be at their best when playing for her. She was as critical as she was attentive; yet if a performance was executed with finesse and skill—and if she had been moved as well as amused—she could be a most appreciative spectator. She let them know when they had pleased her, and they were gratified.

From the plays chosen for court performances over the years, it can be seen that Elizabeth's interests were varied. Shakespeare's *A Midsummer Night's Dream*, *Comedy of Errors*, and *Two Gentlemen of Verona*, all romantic comedies, are believed to have been acted at court toward the end of her reign. These plays, with their broad strokes of earthy humor, apparently pleased Elizabeth as much as they delighted the groundlings. And she enjoyed tragedies as well —not only for their violence and swift action but for their

At a time when acting companies were touring provincial England, troupes of comedians were roaming about the Continent, attracting spectators wherever they stopped.

themes and morals and their subtleties of characterization.

Shortly after the court performance of 1592, the ban on play production was lifted, but only temporarily. By February, 1593, the deaths from the plague had risen again, and another closing was decreed. This shutdown lasted more than a year, until the plague had run its course.

It is likely that the company Shakespeare worked for went on tour in the summer of 1593, but there is no evidence that he went with them. Perhaps he was not needed among the small complement of players who were to travel. Or perhaps, encouraged by the success and unexpected popularity of his first narrative poem, he chose to stay behind to work on a second, *The Rape of Lucrece*.

No significant new plays appeared during the plague years. The acting companies, making use of what plays they had, toured the towns and hamlets where even the most familiar works seemed like novel entertainment. Some rewriting of the old works was done, however, and passages considered too sophisticated for provincial audiences were removed. And because touring companies were small, there were also attempts to cut down the number of parts to be played.

Although scripts were no problem for the touring players, money was. High traveling expenses and smaller audiences made touring less profitable for the companies than performing in London. Often the wages of hired men had to be cut in half when a company went on the road.

Competition also added to the touring actors' woes. Some large communities had groups of amateur actors with standards high enough to rival the work of the London troupes. In other towns there were fairs and folk plays. And throughout England there were traveling entertainers of various sorts who could always command a crowd: Turkish dancers, tumblers and acrobats, mountebanks. For all the backbreaking toil the touring players endured, their audiences were often sparse and their profits few.

Moving from town to town, most of the members of a company traveled on foot; only the chief actors could afford to hire horses. At the end of each day's journey, the players looked forward to the welcome shelter of an inn. There they ate heartily and enjoyed a night's rest before resuming their travel in the morning.

The horse-borne members of a troupe, mud-spattered and caked with dust, left their mounts in the innyard. There the weary horses were walked, rubbed, and bedded down by servants. The senior actors were probably not the first guests to be attended to, however, for the servants had sharp eyes for men of means—or lack of it. Few of the senior actors could tip lavishly. Fewer still could afford private chambers where a fire would be lighted for them, where their soiled boots might be pulled off and taken to be cleaned, and where supper might be served to them in quiet solitude.

Usually, all the actors ate together. Some nights they dined with the innkeeper if he was a merry enough fellow to enjoy their company, or worldly enough to have seen plays performed at one of the London theatres. But more often they simply took potluck at the common table and hoped that another traveler, richer than they, would pay the musicians to play while they had their supper.

As more and more companies took to the road, fewer people seemed interested in seeing them. Local authorities did not encourage attendance at these touring performances. In many towns the presence of actors was considered a hazard, linked with outbreaks of riot, disease, and

The Earl of Pembroke, patron of one of the touring companies, appears here in a flat, plumed hat.

petty crime. Nor were the traveling players particularly welcome at the universities. At that time Oxford and Cambridge were especially strict in keeping the players outside their gates. The academicians took a scholarly view of drama; they considered the work of the traveling companies to be not only unscholarly but worthless and vulgar.

The summer of 1593 was disastrous for a great many touring companies. And when a company was ruined, life became more insecure for actors in the others. In September of that year, Philip Henslowe, business manager for Lord Strange's Men, wrote to Edward Alleyn, who was leading that company on its tour: "As for my Lord of Pembroke's [Men] . . . they are all at home and have been these five or six weeks, for they cannot save their charges with travel, as I hear, and were fain [obliged] to pawn their apparel."

The letter suggests that Pembroke's Men could not even earn back their expenses while on the road, and that they had been forced to sell their costumes to finance a return to London. Their tour had ended abruptly in August, and the company had been dissolved. Other acting companies collapsed under the economic strain as the plague persisted. Many actors were stranded in the country, far from their London homes. Some of them joined other companies, but many took odd jobs—anything that would earn them money to feed their families. Returning to London was not a pleasant prospect, for the playhouses were still closed, and the city lived under a veil of fear that was to last for some time. Until this fear had passed, all that remained of the theatre in London was a memory.

Seated on thickly cushioned stools, no doubt to ease the pain of a long day's ride, the noblemen in this woodcut are served supper in an inn.

A typical English inn was built around a rectangular courtyard. Here, where horses were brushed and bags unloaded, traveling players often acted their plays. Elizabethan playhouses owed much to the innyard theatres. In each of them, spectators could stand in the yard or sit in the galleries above.

69

THE GLOBE

By springtime, 1594, the plague epidemic had played itself out. The theatres reopened, but many of the acting companies that had existed before the plague were no more. The displaced players reorganized, and among the new companies they formed were two that would dominate the English theatre scene for the rest of the Elizabethan Age.

One of these companies was headed by Edward Alleyn, who had been a prominent member of Lord Strange's Men. The company's patron was Lord Charles Howard, a former naval commander who was now Lord High Admiral of England. Thus this group, which occupied the Rose, was called the Lord Admiral's Men.

The other group, whose patron was Lord Hunsdon, the Lord Chamberlain, was called the Lord Chamberlain's Men. One of Lord Hunsdon's official functions was to supervise court entertainment; naturally the company that received the patronage of a man in this position would be particularly favored by the Crown.

The Lord Chamberlain's Men was the first company to which Shakespeare is known to have belonged. Evidence of his association is found in the receipts of the Lord Chamberlain's Men, who performed at Greenwich Palace during the Christmas season of 1594. Shakespeare was one of three actors specifically listed in the receipts. The others were James Burbage's son Richard, soon to be recognized as the leading player of the Elizabethan theatre, and Will Kempe, the most popular comic actor of his time. Each of these men was a sharer in the acting company, for only senior actors would have been named for payment.

The year 1594 may well have marked a turning point in Shakespeare's professional life. By that time he had

The Globe Theatre, with its thatch and plaster exterior, is in the foreground of a scale model of London built for the English film Henry V.

begun enjoying some success as a playwright, and his reputation as a poet was well established. He had to choose then between furthering his literary career or returning to the theatre. The decision he made suggests that though he had a poet's pen, his interests were focused on the stage: nearly everything he wrote after 1594 was for performance rather than publication. He remained with the group that formed the Lord Chamberlain's Men for the rest of his career.

In 1594 London had three permanent playhouses, each

The most renowned players on the Elizabethan stage included John Lowin (top), who acted with Shakespeare and Burbage; the versatile Will Kempe, a nimble dancer (bottom) as well as a comedian; and Edward Alleyn (above), an actor who headed the Lord Admiral's Men.

with a resident company of professional players. But the Lord Chamberlain's Men did not have a theatre of their own for some time. In the next four years they made use of The Theatre and also the Curtain, and possibly the Swan, which was completed in 1595 in Southwark near the Rose. But when the company was preparing to begin its first season in the fall of 1594, no playhouse was available —only an inn.

It was called the Cross Keys Inn, and as it had been used in the past as a theatre, it was suitably equipped for performances. The actors made plans to lease it, but their plans fell through. The Cross Keys was situated inside London, and the Lord Mayor still opposed the performance of plays within the city walls. It was only after the Lord Chamberlain himself intervened that the players received permission to use the inn. But they had to agree to certain conditions: they would not parade through the streets, blowing horns and beating drums to advertise their performances; they would give some of each day's earnings to the poor in the parish; and they would start performances at two in the afternoon so the younger members of the audience could reach home before dark.

Clearly the company still needed a new theatre of its own, in an area without restrictions. But four years would pass before the need would be filled. During that time, the company's leading playwright, William Shakespeare, gained such respect from his associates that when a new theatre finally was built, he became one of its planners.

He was regarded as an accomplished craftsman—and he considered himself no more than that. Indeed, he made no effort to have his plays published; he apparently shared the contemporary opinion that plays were not literature. Ben Jonson, another young Elizabethan playwright, was of a different mind. Fortunately for modern readers, Jonson was eccentric enough to believe that his writing should be preserved. Meticulously he prepared the texts of all his plays for the printer. What he submitted included all the revisions that had been made when his plays were performed, and he added pages that listed the cast of characters and the dates of performance; in some cases he included the names of actors who had played the various parts. In 1616, when he was past forty, Jonson published a volume of his plays—a step that earned him the ridicule of his contemporaries.

Although the drafts of Shakespeare's plays were not for publication, they were polished nonetheless. He worked

Lord Hunsdon, Queen Elizabeth's Lord Chamberlain, was the patron of Shakespeare's acting company.

Soldier players in Shakespeare's history plays dressed like these English troops—with half-armor, high-crested helmets, and short, full breeches known as trunk hose.

swiftly and with a truly professional skill. Two of his fellow players, John Heminges and Henry Condell, were later to say, "We have scarce received from him a blot in his papers." Shakespeare's plays had to be very tightly worked out in his mind before being committed to paper, if only because his actor's life kept him so busy that there was not time to make extensive revisions. Neat and carefully prepared, many of his plays were surprisingly long, requiring more than three hours to perform. But since there were not enough daylight hours for such lengthy performances, cuts were necessary, particularly in midwinter.

Romeo and Juliet was one of Shakespeare's first efforts for the Lord Chamberlain's company. As with many Elizabethan plays, the story upon which it was based had originated in Italy some years earlier and was famous throughout Europe. Eventually it reached England in poetic form, and at that point apparently came to Shakespeare's attention. The tragic tale was well known in London, for more than one contemporary poem described the plight of the star-crossed young lovers. Even so, he added a prologue to his play to tell audiences exactly what it was about.

The play's characters were as familiar as the plot: the hot-blooded hero, the rash but noble heroine, the slightly ribald nurse, and the bumbling priest. But Shakespeare breathed such glowing life into these characters that they seemed totally new.

Even in his patriotic history plays, Shakespeare was able to characterize the dead kings and queens of English history and present them as believable human beings. Shakespeare's ability to handle historic themes had improved steadily since his early years in London when he had written *Henry VI*. Now as a follow-up to that trilogy, which told the story of England's War of the Roses, he wrote *Richard III*, one of the few plays in which his central character was a villain. As source material for this play, and for other plays of the history cycle, Shakespeare used Raphael Holinshed's *Chronicles*. This three-volume reference work, published in 1587, was the most reliable and up-to-date historical effort of the period. Dipping repeatedly into the *Chronicles*, Shakespeare wrote *Richard II* in about 1596, the two-part *Henry IV* a year or so later, and finally *Henry V*.

With these successful plays Shakespeare came into prominence. Now he was ready to step into a commanding position in the world of the theatre.

By 1598 James Burbage, owner of The Theatre, was dead, and the lease on the land where this playhouse stood had expired. Burbage's sons, Cuthbert and Richard, had wrangled for months with the landowner, Giles Allen, in the hope of persuading him to grant a new lease. But Allen refused; he did not want a playhouse on his land indefinitely.

The Burbages did not accept this defeat graciously. They leased a plot of land in an area known as the Bankside, on the south bank of the Thames, and made plans to build a new theatre there. Money for this enterprise was put up by the brothers themselves along with five members of the Lord Chamberlain's company, including William Shakespeare. Once Shakespeare had been a sharer; now he was an owner. The new playhouse would be partly his.

A few days after Christmas, 1598, while Giles Allen was away on a holiday, The Theatre was torn down and its lumber carted across the river to the Bankside. When Allen learned of this he was furious, and he immediately brought suit against the stock company. He lost his case, however; the terms of the lease originally signed by James Burbage permitted the playhouse to be demolished and stripped of its timber.

The dismantling activity was recorded in the charges brought against the Burbages by Giles Allen. According to Allen's complaint:

The said Cuthbert Burbage . . . with the said Richard Burbage and . . . diverse other persons to the number of twelve, to your subject unknown, did about the eight and twentieth day of December [1598] . . . riotously assemble themselves together . . . armed with diverse and many unlawful and offensive weapons, as namely swords, daggers, bills, axes, and such like. And so armed did then repair unto the said Theatre, and then and there armed as aforesaid in a very riotous, outrageous, and forcible manner, and contrary to the laws of your Highness' realm, attempted to pull down the said Theatre . . .

It was a riotous scene, as the complainant suggested, and Shakespeare as an interested party may have witnessed it. Though he may not have taken part in dismantling The Theatre, he was personally involved in the design and construction of the new playhouse. Like the other actors who held part ownership, he had much to contribute after his many years of playing in the older theatres.

The Bankside was a good location, convenient to Londoners who by the thousands poured across the river by rowboat or on foot over London Bridge. The district on the Thames' south bank was fast becoming an entertainment center, for it was outside the control of city authorities. The Rose and the Swan theatres were there, as well as the bull- and bear-baiting rings, the archery butts in St. George's Fields, and many taverns.

The new playhouse was called the Globe. Its emblem, which appeared on a sign in front of the main entrance, showed the Greek god Hercules supporting a world globe on his shoulders. Also inscribed on the emblem was a Latin motto, *Totus mundus agit histrionem* ("All the world's a stage").

Like The Theatre, after which it was modeled, the Globe was many sided, with curving galleries on three levels surrounding an open yard. The building had a wooden frame and a plaster exterior, and though most of it was open to the sky, there was a thatched roof over the galleries and the tiring room. Scholars have pieced together an image of the Globe, but no plan or architectural drawing has ever been found.

There is reason to believe that the stage of the Globe jutted out into the yard and that most of the audience stood or sat on three sides of the actors. This was the usual Elizabethan design. But it has never been clearly established whether the stage apron was tapered or rectangular. Nor is it known how many doors there were on stage to serve as entrances and exits for the actors. A study of the plays presented at the Globe reveals that there must have

Few contemporary pictures of the Globe survive. This seventeenth-century sketch is believed accurate, though the building is undersized.

Richard Burbage was considered one of the finest actors on the Elizabethan stage. It was for him Shakespeare wrote Othello, King Lear, *and* Hamlet. *A man of many talents, Burbage was an artist as well as a performer. He may have painted this oil portrait himself.*

been at least two doors, for more than one Elizabethan play required two actors to come on stage simultaneously. Whether a third door existed, no one knows. Another uncertainty involves the use of the enclosure, which was often called the inner stage. Whole scenes may have been played there. Or, more likely, it may have been used for short transitional scenes or as a place in which one actor might hide from another. How deep was the enclosure? how wide? No one can really say.

One argument against believing the enclosure was a separate acting area is that Elizabethan theatre audiences did not require the use of different stage areas to show changes of locale. Even the groundlings knew that each time a group of players entered the stage, the setting had probably changed. The playing area that had been a forest could suddenly become a courtyard or a street. The audience knew by the flow of action just what the setting was supposed to be. And often a playwright would help by

TEXT CONTINUED ON PAGE 81

The afternoon sun's slanting rays fill the Globe with light. From within the curtained enclosure an actor appears on the main stage to start the performance. He is to recite the prologue, which will quiet the audience and at the same time introduce them to the characters and situations in the play. The wealthy spectators in the upstairs galleries sit quietly, awaiting the players. Not so the groundlings; they move about, gossiping with one another in the final moments of hubbub while pickpockets hurry in their search for fat purses. And a vendor (far left) continues hawking his fruit and cakes. This representation of a scene in the Globe was painted by a modern artist. It is based on a scale model of the theatre and reflects what are believed to be the design and actual dimensions.

79

Because Shakespeare and Ben Jonson were good friends, it is possible that this picture of them was painted from life. Yet many experts question it, stating only that it was painted in 1603 by a Dutchman, Karel van Mander.

TEXT CONTINUED FROM PAGE 77

having a character identify the locale as soon as he came on stage. "Well, this is the forest of Arden," says Rosalind at the opening of a scene in Shakespeare's *As You Like It*.

In Shakespeare's *Henry V*, the limitations of the stage were most pointedly felt, for within the scope of the play are the camps of both the English and the French and the entire Battle of Agincourt. Thus Shakespeare felt obliged to write a prologue in which a character named Chorus calls upon the audience to use its imagination so the scene can be visualized.

> Suppose within the girdle of these walls
> Are now confin'd the mighty monarchies,
> Whose high-upreared and abutting fronts
> The perilous narrow ocean parts asunder.

And later he urges them to

> Think when we talk of horses that you see them
> Printing their proud hoofs i' the receiving earth.

On the day of a performance at the Globe, the flag atop the tower of the tiring room was raised to call the people to the theatre. And a variety of people came: apprentices, noblemen, gentlemen, authors, ladies, women of the streets —mixed with curious foreigners and country justices who had come to London for a term of court. Audiences were nearly always a cross section of the diversified London populace. All hurried to pay their money and find their places before the trumpet sounded.

Prices ranged from a penny to a shilling. A penny bought standing room in the yard, the choicest vantage points being either at the front or at the sides of the projecting stage. For more money a spectator could sit in one of the three curving galleries. And near the stage, on each side, were boxes called lords' rooms which noblemen could rent. For the more fashionable playgoers whose first wish was to gain the attention of other elegant and influential persons, stools could be rented for a high price and placed on the sides or front edges of the stage itself.

Three blasts of the trumpet hushed the hubbub in the theatre, and the performance began. The players entered from the doors at the back of the stage. The tempo of their acting was fast, and they performed an entire play without interruption. There were no long waits between scenes, no curtains to descend and cut off the actors from the audience.

It was as if the spectators were invited to become personally involved in the action, for many of the actors' witty comments were played directly to them in the form of asides, and soliloquies were often delivered from the forward edge of the stage. The groundlings easily became restless, of course, if a play failed to hold their interest, and often they chatted among themselves to relieve their boredom. It was only when a performance was really bad that their rudeness became more aggressive. Hurling insults and tossing ripe fruit, they drove the actors from the stage. The groundlings, though uneducated, were avid playgoers.

The first performance at the Globe took place in the summer of 1599. Within a year, not to be outdone by the Lord Chamberlain's company, the Lord Admiral's Men built a new theatre for their sole use. This one, erected in the suburbs north of London, was called the Fortune.

The design of the Fortune was very close to that of the Globe. Philip Henslowe and Edward Alleyn, who financed the structure, employed the same master carpenter. And in their building contract they stipulated that the Fortune was "to be in all other [contrivances], conveyances, fashions, thing, and things, effected, finished, and done according to the manner and fashion of the said house called the Globe." Shakespeare's theatre was already successful enough to be copied.

Two years after the Globe had opened, old John Shakespeare died, and the deed to the family property in Stratford passed to his oldest son, William. So too did the coat of arms, which had finally been awarded to John Shakespeare in 1596. The design that was authorized by the Office of Heralds seems to have no particular knightly significance, but its meaning is unmistakable. Across the shield runs a diagonal black band on which is a silver spear; the crest of the shield consists of a falcon standing on a wreath and holding another spear. Though the coat of arms is not a work of great beauty, it is indeed appropriate to the name Shakespeare.

As head of the Shakespeare family, thirty-seven-year-old William became responsible for all its property. This, in addition to his father's home on Henley Street, included a purchase he himself had made in 1597—New Place, the second largest house in town. New Place became Shakespeare's official residence in Stratford, and there his wife, Anne, lived with their two daughters. With a family estate and the coat of arms left by his father, his prestige in Stratford was now higher than had once seemed possible. To his neighbors, who were little concerned with his success in London, he was known as William Shakespeare, Gentleman.

This version of the Shakespeare coat of arms was copied from a crude sketch that appeared on the document that awarded the honor.

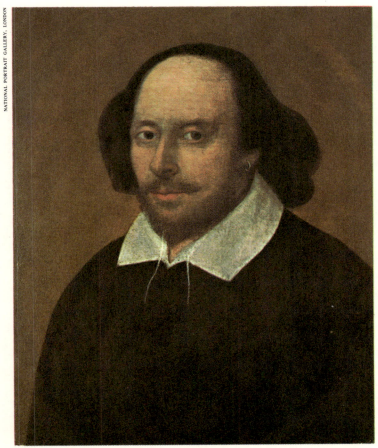

An engraver, George Vertue, did the above sketch of *New Place* "by memory" in 1737, twenty-two years before the house was leveled. It is the only contemporary drawing of Shakespeare's home that is said to be authentic. Nothing so positive can be said of the picture at left. Supposedly it is a portrait of the playwright, and it may have been painted by his colleague Burbage.

THE EUROPEAN STAGE

Early in Queen Elizabeth's reign an ambassador sent her a careful report on Italian theatricals. For Italy was then the source of most new ideas in the arts, the center of the Renaissance. Yet it was in England, with the building of public playhouses and the writing of the great Elizabethan dramas, that the Renaissance theatre reached its peak. The illustrations on these and the following four pages show several colorful European stages that either mirrored or influenced the changing English theatre. At right is an Italian pageant-wagon from about 1580, which, like its English equivalent, was used to carry one scene of a religious drama through a town. Below, a magnificent procession winds around a square in Brussels in 1615. On each wagon a separate playlet of religious or political significance is acted. At lower right, for example, Brussels' loveliest maidens are arranged as the court of the goddess Diana in an effort to honor their ruler, Archduchess Isabella.

85

In the dining hall of an Austrian castle, a troupe of masked actors dance, sing, and declaim fo

...he benefit of the feasting guests. This form of court entertainment was common throughout Europe.

The woodsy scene at left was set up for a ballet at a French court. Especially notable is the stage at rear; behind the arches is a curtain painted to indicate distant vistas. At right is a play staged in a local French assembly hall about 1588. Three innovations are candles used for footlights, a front curtain that closed between scenes, and a gallery for musicians (upper left)

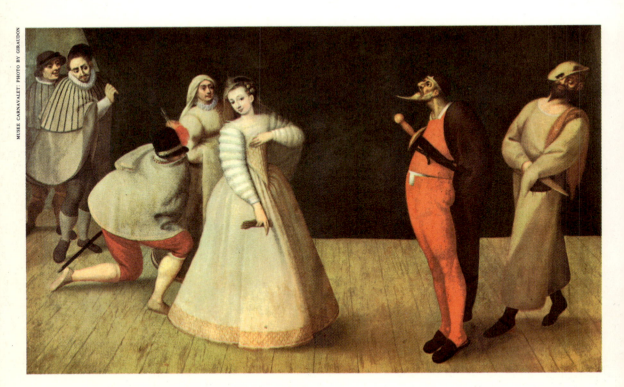

This sixteenth-century painting shows a troupe of Italian comedians who are performing on a high stage erected in a market place. The old man is Pantalone, a villain traditionally dressed in peculiar stocking-trousers.

90

REBELLION OF A FAVORITE

The English stage failed to prosper in the 1590's despite the appearance of new dramatic works by Shakespeare, Ben Jonson, and Thomas Nashe. This was a time when England was passing through a number of grave perils, including war with Spain and rebellion in Ireland; and the wonder is not that the Elizabethan theatre declined, but that the theatre, and its newly established profession of playwriting, survived at all.

By 1590 the Puritans had increased their influence in the country's provinces, and the impact of their sober beliefs was being felt more strongly in London. The Lord Mayor himself undertook a campaign which had but one object: to rid his city of those beds of sin, the playhouses. Plays, charged the mayor, were "a special cause of corrupting youth, containing nothing but unchaste matter, lascivious devices . . . and ungodly practices." He was concerned further that if the content of the plays did not corrupt innocent theatregoers, the other members of the audience surely would. Thieves, atheists, and other such riffraff, he maintained, were the people most likely to be found attending the theatre.

Emphasizing this danger and the ever-present possibility of the plague's recurrence, London authorities continued to rail against the theatre. But nothing so simple as prudishness or hygiene lay at the heart of their concern. They actually feared that the plays were a menace to the security of the nation.

The Church, the law, and the Crown were all subjects Elizabethan playwrights would have liked to portray, but they were restrained by fear of the laws. To keep their

Two threats to the peace and cultural growth of Elizabethan England were the handsome Earl of Essex (left), whose escapades shook the nation, and Puritans (like the gossips above), who disapproved of art and the theatre.

witty thrusts under control, licensing had always been strict. Now the process of screening plays was tightened, and players found that the authorities were ready to take drastic measures to keep dangerous sentiments off the stage. *The Isle of Dogs*, which was presented at the Swan in 1596, was considered so offensive and slanderous that three of its actors were jailed. One of these men, Ben Jonson, was also suspected of having written part of the play. Thomas Nashe, the writer responsible for much of it, only escaped arrest by leaving town.

Soon afterward, a government order was issued that halted the production of all plays and marked all playhouses for destruction. Yet the theatre professionals with whom Shakespeare was associated were not dismayed: theatres had been closed many times before. The actors

As ladies weep and gentlemen in tall hats look on disinterestedly, Mary Queen of Scots is beheaded. Her execution did little to decide who would inherit the English crown.

went on tour, leaving behind them the dark and unused playhouses. They took with them the continuing hope for better days.

Their optimism seemed to be justified when the theatres were reopened in late fall of 1596. But the audiences were disappointingly sparse; by the end of April, 1597, the expected spring upsurge of attendance had not come. Why were Londoners suddenly so cautious with their pennies, and so unwilling to make the pleasant cross-river jaunt to the theatres?

The Lord Mayor and members of the London council may have congratulated themselves on having dampened popular enthusiasm for the theatre. But their actions had had very little effect. What had happened was actually more the result of economics and politics than censorship. England had recently sunk into a state of economic depression. Adding to the financial pinch, which was felt by nearly everyone, taxes had been raised severely to keep the government from bankruptcy. As a result, opposition to the policies of Queen Elizabeth was on the rise. The occasional mumbles of discontent that had issued from the people during the previous decade had become loud shouts of protest.

England's sorry financial state, which so adversely affected the theatre, was only one of the problems that concerned the people. Another problem involved the royal succession, which had remained unsettled since Elizabeth came to the throne. The issue had provoked a national crisis in 1587 when Elizabeth's cousin, Mary Queen of Scots, was beheaded. The execution was carried out by Elizabeth's supporters, statesmen who wanted to insure that neither Mary nor any other Roman Catholic would succeed to the throne of Protestant England. But putting Mary to death did nothing to ease the problem—another crisis of succession might erupt at any moment.

Elizabeth, being unmarried, had no direct heirs. It was up to her to name her successor voluntarily or to accept one who was forced upon her. This last possibility was in the minds of a group of men who in 1599 concocted a daring scheme. They planned to lead an uprising against the Queen.

Shakespeare, as it happened, played a small and unwitting role in this brief court rebellion. The major player in the uprising was Robert Devereux, the second Earl of Essex. Even without embellishment the story of

The Earl of Leicester, Essex's stepfather, appears here as an able-bodied, partially armored knight.

his rise and fall is one of the tragedies of English history.

Essex had spent the first portion of his life in the shadow of his stepfather, the Earl of Leicester. That audacious and powerful noble was undoubtedly the man who came closest of any of the Queen's courtiers to winning her heart. Other men may have held her confidence—advisers like Sir Francis Walsingham and Lord Burleigh—but no one held her affection as Leicester had during his lifetime. When he died in 1588 Elizabeth took pains, in an almost widowlike way, to preserve the final note she had received from him, scrawling on it the words "His last letter."

Just before Leicester's death, the Queen had taken kindly notice of his twenty-two-year-old stepson, the Earl of Essex. She had suggested that the young man move into Leicester House and become better acquainted with court life. Essex was flattered by the attention, but he was worried that his stepfather might disapprove. His letter to Leicester about the opportunity was, therefore, tactful and deferential: "I will forbear to do [so] till I know your Lordship's pleasure, except the Queen force me to it." After Leicester's death, however, the young man moved into the sumptuous residence and eventually renamed it Essex House. At the same time he moved into the center of Queen Elizabeth's public and private life.

Less robust than Leicester, but abounding in charm, Essex has been called a beautifully sad young man. His hair was reddish gold and his face expressed both sensitivity and intelligence. Fresh from the halls of Cambridge University, but already wise to the ways of the world, he seemed destined to capture the Queen's favor. He had a rare gift that enabled him to gain the confidence and affection of others. With astonishing swiftness, the young Earl achieved a status almost as great as that of his late stepfather.

Essex's only serious rivals to political prominence were Sir Walter Raleigh, whose rise had been similarly swift, and Robert Cecil, the son of Elizabeth's trusted Lord Burleigh. Essex easily eclipsed Raleigh, who was no longer popular with the Queen, and no doubt enjoyed the victory. Robert Cecil, the other political rival, was a young man whose mental powers approached genius. But as he was a hunchback, he could never gain the Queen's personal affections. Essex stood alone as her favorite.

At first, he was always with the Queen at court. When she rode in state, he walked beside her as her Master

2

4

Before and after the death of Mary Queen of Scots, Protestant English-men feared Catholic attempts to depose or murder Elizabeth. To counter the suspected plots against Elizabeth's life, the aid of her two closest advisers was sought. The two noblemen, Sir Francis Walsingham and Lord Burleigh, are shown flanking her throne in the large picture above. The other pictures represent some of the intrigues they detected or foiled. 1. Thomas Stukely (kneeling) conspires with the pope (left) and the king of Spain to dethrone Elizabeth. 2. Dr. William Parry is prevented from killing the Queen even though he bears the promise of papal absolu-tion. 3. Two noblemen seek priestly approval for a plot by the Earls of Westmorland and Northumberland to give Mary of Scotland the crown. 4. The young man with a vial is one of a group of squires who plotted to poison Queen Elizabeth. These pictures are all from a book written by George Carleton, Bishop of Chichester, early in the seventeenth century.

95

On a horse whose plumed headdress matches his own, and carrying a short staff called a truncheon, the Earl of Essex personifies the daring and elegance of Elizabethan nobility. Always exuberant, often arrogant, Essex could lead troops and compose verse with equal dash.

Essex reached the height of his success in 1596 with the sacking of Cadiz, shown in the woodcut at right. Commanding a fleet of more than eighty ships, he attacked the Spanish port and left it in flames.

of the Horse. At palace parties his was a welcome presence, and when the long public day was over, he was a dear companion to her at chess or cards. Elizabeth bound him to her court, and from his fellow courtiers he gathered about him a group of loyal and devoted men. The Earl of Southampton was Essex's most intimate friend. However, Robert Cecil, who was aware of the young nobleman's gifts and aspirations, was cautious and remained aloof.

Essex was not a fine and skilled courtier; perhaps, in a curious way, this was one of his attractions for Elizabeth. He spoke his mind and never concealed his personal pride. His design for social advancement was grandiose, and his arrogance was unbridled. Although his counsel was considered valuable, his directness was often less prudent than either his Queen or his noble colleagues could tolerate. When rebuffed, he would retire and sulk, with magnificent effect, for days or sometimes weeks.

He was restless, eager to earn glory. He sailed against Spain with Sir Francis Drake. He fought in France. And in what was probably his greatest triumph, he led English ships in a surprise attack on Cadiz in June, 1596, and reduced the Spanish city to ashes. He had become a national hero, which heightened his ego but did not endear him further to his fellow courtiers. Each time he returned to England, outbursts of jealousy and antagonism marked his relationship with other members of the court. He was so self-assured that not even the Queen was spared his wrath if she happened to differ with him. Yet he remained her favorite. She chided him for his behavior, humored his rivals in their grievances against him, and then coaxed him back to her again.

As time passed, the friction between Elizabeth and Essex increased. Power, and a hunger for more of it, began to have a corrupting effect on the young nobleman. Essex became preoccupied with the question of the royal succession. To whom would the crown pass if the Queen should suddenly die? Many people believed the problem could best be solved by naming Scotland's King James VI as her successor. He was the son of Mary Queen of Scots, and his succession was intolerable to Elizabeth. Still, James seemed the likeliest candidate.

In 1597 there was trouble in Ireland. Resentment against English rule had broken into open rebellion under the leadership of the Earl of Tyrone. A new English commander in chief was needed, a man capable of crushing the rebellion before it had swelled into full-scale war. The Queen called a meeting of her councilors to select such a man. Essex argued that the new commander be "some prime man of the nobility, strong in power, honor, and wealth, in favor with military men, who had been before general of an army." All eyes were on the speaker. Essex, perhaps without realizing it, had advanced his own candidacy.

He was guilty, no doubt, of believing himself braver and nobler than any of his peers, but his desire to fight in Ireland had other causes. Elizabeth's continued pampering of him placed a limit on his personal power, as did his ceaseless involvement in petty disputes at court. The best way for him to remain a popular hero would be to leave the country again on a mission for his Queen.

Essex was aware, no doubt, that failure to defeat Tyrone would ruin his career. But as the road to glory seemed to start in Ireland, he had to take the risk. He rounded up a troop of crack officers to accompany him and bickered at length over the authority that his appointment brought him. Then on March 27, 1599, he left London. He crossed the stormy Irish Sea in fog and mist; his thoughts were nearly as turbulent as the weather.

Essex was not long in Ireland before he began writing to his Queen that the English forces were short of men and were in particular need of horses. His requests went unheeded, which prompted him to write sternly and bitterly to the royal council: "I must save myself by protestation that it is not Tyrone and the Irish rebellion that amazeth me, but to see myself sent on such an errand, at such a time, with so little comfort and ability from the court of England to effect that I go about."

The Queen responded angrily in a series of letters that charged him with needless delays and inaction, and prohibited him from the shores of England "until the Northern action be tried." Humiliated by the Queen's merciless snipings, his army demoralized by skirmishes with Tyrone's superior forces, Essex chose what many historians believe was the only course open to him. He attempted a truce with Tyrone.

They met at the ford of Bellaclinthe in the river Lagan. They shouted to each other over the roar of rushing water—Essex from the bank, Tyrone from the ford itself. They pondered each other's terms, and some time later, on September 8, they reached an agreement. Their truce could be canceled only after two weeks' notice by either side.

The cessation of hostilities was beneficial to both sides, but it was perhaps more advantageous to Tyrone. He could delay further action until assistance from Spain arrived. The English also gained time by the truce—time to regroup their ragged forces and bring in fresh troops from England, if they chose to do so. But they did not.

TEXT CONTINUED ON PAGE 102

By agreeing to a truce with Essex, the wily Tyrone outwitted England again. Once before, simply to gain time, he had surrendered to the Earl of Ormonde. In this woodcut, Tyrone kneels before Ormonde, the English commander in Ireland.

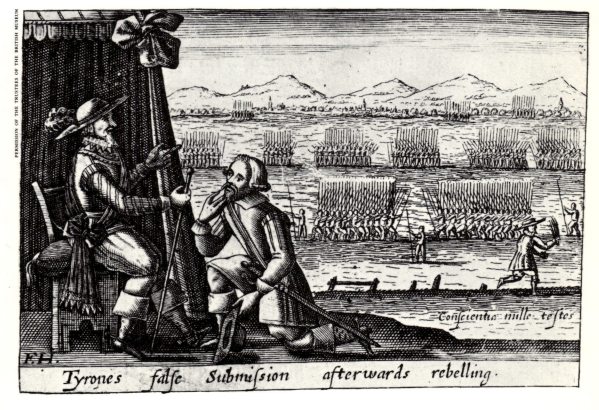

Conscientia mille testes

F.H.

Tyrones false Submission afterwards rebelling.

99

Cahir Castle taken by the Earle of Essex in anno 1599

In 1599 Essex captured the rebel stronghold of Cahir Castle in Leinster, Ireland. His soldiers can be seen on shore shooting at the island fortification. This woodcut is from a book published in 1633 that chronicled the long, bitter conflict between England and Ireland. Essex's victory at Cahir provided a temporary lift to the flagging English spirit, but his effort to subdue the Irish rebels was doomed to fail eventually.

101

The hero of Shakespeare's Hamlet *is as passionate and unstable as Essex. In an eighteenth-century engraving of a scene from the play, Prince Hamlet sits moodily at the feet of Ophelia as King Claudius, his uncle, and Queen Gertrude watch players re-enact Claudius' "foul and most unnatural murder" of the old king, Hamlet's father.*

TEXT CONTINUED FROM PAGE 99

Elizabeth was furious that her commander had made any concessions to the rebels. Essex, in turn, disobeyed her orders and left Ireland, determined to have a face-to-face meeting with the Queen.

He arrived in London early on the morning of September 28. Pausing only to obtain a fresh horse, he rode off to Nonsuch Palace at Cheam, Surrey, where the Queen was then staying. He arrived unannounced and strode unceremoniously into the palace. Spattered with mud, and hot from his hard ride, he burst into the Queen's bedchamber.

She had just arisen. She was unused to receiving courtiers in such an informal state, but though caught unawares, she appeared glad to see him. He knelt and kissed her hand, and she spoke to him graciously, seemingly pleased by his safe return. But by evening her manner had changed radically. After a lengthy meeting with her councilors, many of whom relished an opportunity to reprimand

Essex, the Queen became convinced that he should be banished from the court. She would not see him, but sent word that he should keep to the chamber assigned him.

Several days after his return, Essex was committed to York House, where he remained in the custody of the lord keeper. For the next year and a half he was virtually a prisoner. Few servants waited on him. Only a handful of friends came to call. In this semi-isolation he became melancholy and was frequently ill. The physicians dispatched to him by the Queen did no good, nor did the bowls of broth sent from her own table. Clergymen were his more welcome visitors. He obtained some relief from his melancholy state by making confession and receiving communion. If he was mentally ill, as some people believed, he had not lost the control of his thoughts or the ability to create deft phrases. A brief letter to Elizabeth read:

> Haste, paper, to that unhappy presence,
> whence only unhappy I am banished.
> Kiss that fair, correcting hand which
> lays new plasters to my lighter hurts
> but to my greatest wound applieth nothing.
> Say thou comest from shaming, languishing,
> despairing
>
> SX [Essex]

Elizabeth may have been sympathetic toward his illness, but she would answer none of his beseeching letters. The Irish had ended the truce, and Tyrone's resistance to English rule continued unchecked. It would do so until 1603 when Lord Mountjoy subdued all of Ireland and forced Tyrone to surrender. Elizabeth blamed Essex for the ugly situation in Ireland. Although he felt guiltless, his pride had been wounded; he was forced now into a final, desperate act.

Goaded by illness and the Queen's censure, and deeply in debt, Essex—no longer a prisoner but excluded from the court—decided to start a rebellion of his own. He would lead the people against their Queen. She would be dethroned, and James VI of Scotland would be her successor.

Early in 1601, Essex completed his plan. He and his party would move simultaneously on the Tower of London and on Whitehall, where the Queen was in residence. More than a hundred men and a small core of nobles were part of the conspiracy, including his faithful friend Southampton. Essex believed that fear and discontent

In 1678 a play about Essex was presented in Paris. This scene from the play shows Elizabeth observing the Earl's last moments.

had made London a tinderbox that needed only a spark to ignite. Essex would provide that spark. When he marched through the streets, he thought, the people would be aroused to join him.

To stir them to this response, Essex's friends asked the Lord Chamberlain's Men to revive that play in which an indecisive monarch relinquishes his throne, Shakespeare's *Richard II*. The actors were reluctant to put on the play. Perhaps they were suspicious that its production might be put to some evil use. They tried to beg off, stating that such an old play would hardly draw the large audience required to make the production feasible. But when Essex's friends offered to supplement the box-office proceeds with an outright payment of forty shillings,

An eighteenth-century engraving records the climactic event of the career of Essex: after leading an unsuccessful attempt to overthrow the Queen, the unfortunate young nobleman opens his gate and gives himself up to Elizabeth's guards.

the actors could not refuse. A performance of *Richard II* was set for the afternoon of February 7.

It is not known how the play was received; no doubt the Essex faction was in attendance and loudly cheered the abdication scene. But the performance did nothing to foment revolt. The next day, Essex and his followers—now nearly two hundred strong—rushed through the streets, their swords concealed in their cloaks. They implored the citizens to arm and march against the Queen. But no one stirred.

Essex rode to the home of the sheriff, who had promised to support the uprising. Essex found the house empty. The sheriff had changed his mind, and had fled through the back door. A herald arrived on the scene, and from him Essex learned that the Queen had sent messengers throughout the city declaring that her former favorite had become a traitor. There was only one course as the day closed; he would have to retreat to Essex House and there make a final stand.

His forces were dwindling. Many of his friends abandoned him; still others were seized as they rode after their leader. There were skirmishes with firearms, and two or three bullets tore through the hat Essex wore. But he reached home in safety and barricaded the doors and windows for the siege to come. Despite his weariness and an all-consuming sense of failure, he had the presence of mind to thrust the paper that bore his supporters' names into the fire.

At first he was determined to die fighting. Then, realizing his cause was lost, he decided he would surrender and stand trial for his actions. His sword gleamed in the torchlight as he handed it over. He was taken to the Tower.

Eleven days later, on February 19, Essex and Southampton were brought to trial in Westminster Hall. Essex pleaded not guilty, but his plea made no difference. The prosecuting lawyers built an unshakable case; he was convicted and condemned. His last gracious act was to request leniency for his friend Southampton.

During the next five days, while he was locked in the Tower, his mind was in a turmoil. He unburdened himself of a series of confessions. He admitted that he had plotted for the succession of James VI, but, he said, his intentions had been good. He declared that he had acted out of concern for his country.

The Queen suffered now as she had years earlier before the death of Mary Queen of Scots. Elizabeth had

This woodcut illustrated a ballad about the Earl of Essex's death.

loved Essex, but he had betrayed her and then had confessed his traitorous acts in writing. Thus he could not be spared, not even by her hand. Execution was inevitable.

On February 25, after a night spent in prayer, Essex was taken to the block on Tower Green. Three clergymen and an armed guard were with him. It was a chilly morning. A small group of nobles, ordered there by the Queen, sat on a bench facing the scaffold. A hundred other spectators stood behind them. Raleigh watched from a window in the Tower.

Essex, clad in black satin and velvet with a white ruff, faced his audience. He removed his black hat. He spoke briefly and took off his gown and ruff. He summoned the executioner and then knelt in the straw before the block and prayed. Rising, he removed his doublet and stood before the audience in a scarlet waistcoat. Then he bowed to the block, prayed again, lay flat on the straw, and adjusted his head.

"Executioner, strike home!" he cried.

There was no movement, no flinching, just three accurate strokes of the axe. Essex was thirty-three, still in his prime. These tragic events occurred in 1601, the year Shakespeare put his hand to the final form of the tragedy of *Hamlet*. Understandably, there are some similarities between the avenging prince of that play and the embittered earl who dominated the events of 1601. Yet in many important respects the characters are totally different.

Essex, like Shakespeare's hero, tried to topple the Crown and brought about his own death in the process. But his motives were small (primarily he was piqued by the Queen's censure) and his actions rash—apparently he never had a clear understanding of even his own objectives. For all his sensitivity, Essex was a man of unreasoned action. Prince Hamlet, on the other hand, was so intellectual that it often seems in the play as if he will never get around to avenging his father's murder.

Shakespeare may have begun writing the play along the lines of a conventional revenge play filled with the violence the Elizabethans loved. Then, as his fascination with Hamlet's character grew, he may have seen in the personalities of certain young courtiers qualities that would make the tragedy more compelling and dramatic. Hamlet, educated at Wittenberg University, became an expression of a new personality on Shakespeare's horizon: the Renaissance man whose trained mind persuaded him to act on reason, not on impulse.

Essex hoped that a performance of Shakespeare's Richard II *would incite Londoners to join his revolt against Elizabeth, for the play is about a king who is forced to give up his crown. In the scene above, a deposed Richard defends himself against the men his successor has sent to kill him.*

SCENES FROM SHAKESPEARE

"A horse! a horse! my kingdom for a horse!" cries the great eighteenth-century actor David Garrick in the painting at left. The memorable words are from act five, scene four, of Shakespeare's *Richard III*, a scene recreating one of the turning points in English history: Richard, unhorsed and out-numbered, loses his throne to Queen Elizabeth's grandfather, Henry VII. Just as this battle marked the beginning of Queen Elizabeth's line of Tudor monarchs, so *Richard III* was a milestone for Shakespeare. It was the dramatic climax of his first history plays, written between 1589 and 1594, in which he began his great dramatic chronicle of English history. The painting below marks the end of that chronicle; it is a scene from Shakespeare's last history play, *Henry VIII*, which he may have written in collaboration with John Fletcher. The episode pictured here is the coronation of Anne Boleyn, Queen Elizabeth's mother. Anne walks beneath a processional canopy, attended by court ladies and the Bishops of London and Winchester (carrying crosiers). Between the writing of *Richard III* and *Henry VIII*, Shakespeare wrote many other plays in which he dramatized different aspects of his England—and of all mankind. There were comedies like *The Merry Wives of Windsor*, romantic tragedies like *Romeo and Juliet*, and great tragedies like *King Lear* and *Macbeth*. Scenes from these plays painted by major English artists of the last century are shown on the next four pages.

In all of Shakespeare's plays the most difficult role to act is that of King Lear, for he is both mighty and mad. At left, in Thomas Sully's painting, Lear rants, "Blow, winds, and crack your cheeks! rage! blow!"

110

Sir John Falstaff, Shakespeare's most comic character, appears in the history plays Henry IV, Parts One and Two *and the comedy* The Merry Wives of Windsor. *Above, in the latter play, he is teased by the merry wives. One of Shakespeare's best-known tragic heroes is Romeo. At left, he declaims: "But soft! what light through yonder window breaks? It is the east, and Juliet is the sun."*

OVERLEAF: *At left in this painting attributed to J.M.W. Turner, the three witches from* Macbeth *chant "Double, double toil and trouble" while Macbeth (right) stands transfixed by a vision of ghostly kings.*

111

The Chariott drawne by foure Horses vpon which Charret stood the Coffin couered w.th purple Veluett and vpon that the representation, The Canapy borne by six Knights.

"Our jewel is from us gone, the valiant knight of chivalry."
A street ballad expressed the grief felt by numberless Englishmen over the death of Essex. Though he had been a
traitor, the people would miss him. So would their Queen.

It was a scant two years from the time of Essex's execution until Elizabeth's own death—a period of uncertainty
and expectancy for the entire nation. To the end of her life
her courtiers hoped that the Queen would break her si-
lence and name her successor. They watched her every
move, noted the state of her health with increasing concern, and tried to make out the pattern of the future.

As for the men of the theatre, they too watched the pageant of the Queen's life and enjoyed two triumphant last
years of her favor. The members of Shakespeare's acting
troupe, who had performed *Richard II* for Essex's men, were
questioned, but received neither punishment nor rebuke.

*Carrying heraldic banners, the
Queen's courtiers accompany her
funeral cortege in this illustration from a manuscript prepared
shortly after her death in 1603.*

Elizabeth was indeed lenient with the followers of her late favorite; only six of them were executed. The Earl of Southampton was let off with a prison term.

The Queen demonstrated that she had lost none of her political ability to choose a middle course between extremes. And court life continued much as before. Despite increasing weariness, Elizabeth continued to ride. She sailed on the royal barge—though she once stumbled, bruising her shin, as she climbed aboard—and only occasionally requested a stick to help her ascend a staircase. Despite the shocks and reversals of the year 1601, she attended the royal amusements without letup. According to persistent tradition, the play she saw at a court performance at Whitehall was *Twelfth Night* by William Shakespeare, presented by the Lord Chamberlain's Men.

By this time Shakespeare's reputation had become solidly established in literary circles. The intellectuals were taking his playwriting seriously, and his name was highly regarded at universities too. In a series of plays written at Cambridge between 1597 and 1601, Shakespeare was given extravagant praise. A character in one of these plays declared, "Let this duncified world esteem Spenser and Chaucer, I'll worship sweet Mr. Shakespeare." He was England's greatest playwright, and his work preserves

Ever the regal figure, Elizabeth was sixty-seven when the portrait at right was painted. She spent her last days of life at Richmond Palace (above).

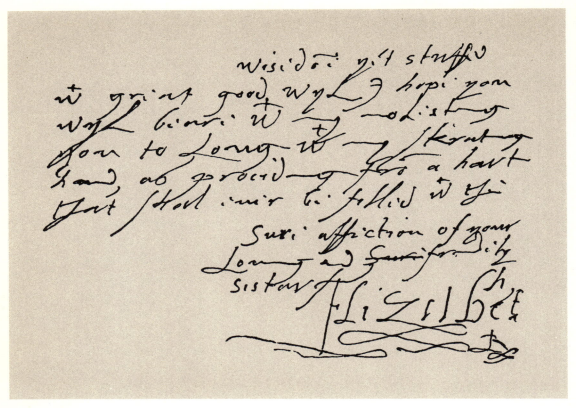

Although slow to name him as her successor, Elizabeth wrote often to James. Above is part of a note, written in her hand, that he received eleven weeks before he was crowned king of England. The end of the message reads, "I hope you wyl beare with my molesting you so long with my [scratching] hand, as prociding from a hart that shal ever be filled with the sure affection of your Loving and frindely sistar, Elizabeth R."

the creative spirit for which the age of Elizabeth is known. Yet as Shakespeare moved into the years of his greatest accomplishments the Queen was failing noticeably.

In October, 1601, Sir John Harington, Elizabeth's godson, was given an audience with her. To him she seemed ill and irritable, like an old lioness at bay. His impression was recorded in a letter he wrote: "Every new message from the city doth disturb her, and she frowns on all the ladies . . . I must not say much even by this trusted and sure messenger; but the many evil plots and designs hath overcome all Her Highness' sweet temper. She walks much in her chamber, and stamps with her feet at ill news, and thrusts her rusty sword at time into the arras [wall tapestry] in great rage . . . But the dangers are over, and yet she always has a sword by her table . . ."

Although the Queen tried to stay young looking, resorting more and more to wigs and cosmetics, her pretense was not convincing to the younger generation at court. She was surrounded now by men who no longer worshiped her. Her beloved Leicester and her trusted Burleigh were dead; other respected contemporaries were dying. The Queen was, in fact, losing touch with the times.

Late in 1601, the House of Commons met to discuss the country's perilous financial condition. It seemed to many of the members that Elizabeth had been too liberal with her economic favors; Parliament agreed to challenge the Queen's right to grant a monopoly to a favorite or a political ally. A monopoly allowed its recipient to profit from the sale of staple articles of the realm—salt, wine, and woolen goods, for instance. It was a kind of open bribe, a way of binding to the Queen the services of some useful public figure. It also meant that money that might have flowed into the kingdom's empty coffers was being stuffed into silk-lined pockets.

The Crown's right to grant monopolies had long been a prerogative that Elizabeth wished to retain. But not wanting to antagonize Parliament, she shrewdly compromised. In a royal proclamation, she established a limit on the granting of monopolies. Thus the Queen averted a struggle with Parliament and kept the authority of the monarchy intact. She also agreed to receive a deputation from the House of Commons at Whitehall Palace, for the members wished to express their gratitude and loyalty.

On the afternoon of November 30, the deputation came. One hundred and fifty members assembled outside the Queen's council chamber. After they had been kept waiting for some time, the great doors were flung open. The group entered, bowed, and knelt.

Elizabeth was in a reflective mood, eager to recall the long years during which she had guided England's destiny. Fervently she addressed the members:

Though God hath raised me high, yet this I account the glory of my crown, that I have reigned with your loves . . . I do not so much rejoice that God hath made me to be a queen, as to be a queen over so thankful a people . . . Of myself I must say this: I never was any greedy, scraping grasper . . . nor yet a waster, my heart was never set upon worldly goods, but only for my subjects' good.

Mercifully, at this point, she asked the men to rise from their aching knees. Then she continued. Her tone was that of a tired old woman, but her speech revealed that the power to manipulate and enchant still was hers:

It is not my desire to live or reign longer than my life and reign shall be for your good. And though you have had, and may have, many mightier and wiser princes sitting in this seat, yet you never had, nor shall have any that will love you better.

TEXT CONTINUED ON PAGE 122

N.Y. PUBLIC LIBRARY, PRINTS DIVISION

Scotland's James VI is seen here after acquiring the title—and the symbols—of James I of England.

119

James appears four times in this depiction of his coronation—first at far left, at the head of

Totus magnatù et principum, dominarù ac virginù comitatu [...]x excipitur.

Chorus insignis musa ferij Occidentalis.

Variæ per urbem jubilatio. ne s.

nouem

Innumera nobilium, aulicorum, et satellitum ante fores templi comorantium turba.

procession, and finally as he receives the mighty sword of state inside Westminster Abbey.

TEXT CONTINUED FROM PAGE 119

The speech was almost over. She concluded it by saying, ". . . I pray you Mr. Comptroller, Mr. Secretary, and you of my council that before these gentlemen go into their counties, you will bring them all to kiss my hand."

One by one they came forward. It was a solemn moment. For many it would be their last audience with the Queen. "We loved her, for she said she did love us," said Harington. These men had heard Elizabeth's "golden speech"; it was referred to for years afterward and remembered through the centuries.

Within months of this gathering, there was evidence that the Queen's memory was failing her and that because of her consuming weariness life held little pleasure for her. She kept up a series of social engagements, however. There was hunting and dancing, and she attended parties

Sentenced to die, Raleigh won his release from prison by promising the King he would find a gold mine in South America without trespassing on Spanish colonies there. As Spain and England were at peace, James vowed he would demand the adventurer's head if Raleigh did not keep his pledge. Inevitably, Raleigh was involved in a fight in which Spanish blood was spilled; his promise to King James was broken. When Raleigh returned to England in 1618, he found that a headsman's axe awaited him (left).

given by her courtiers. Yet there were times, it was whispered, when she sat alone in a darkened room and lamented the loss of Essex.

Elizabeth spent the Christmas season of 1602 at Whitehall, and then in January boarded her barge and moved up the Thames to her palace at Richmond. It was her final journey in a life that had been full of journeys. Once she was settled at Richmond the usual court activities continued. In mid-February, 1603, Shakespeare's company, favored above all others, came to put on a play. The Queen, aged sixty-nine, may have enjoyed it despite her failing powers; it was probably the last play she saw.

She continued to tend to matters of state, however, and to meet with her closest advisers. The Lord Admiral and the Archbishop of Canterbury were frequent visitors. She even saw dignitaries from outside the court. The Venetian ambassador came to protest the raids by English privateers on Venetian shipping. The Queen received him in a gown of silver and white taffeta trimmed with gold. She listened to him and promised to appoint a commission to investigate the matter. As he departed, she voiced concern over the way she had handled the interview. "I know not if I have spoken the Italian well; yet I think so, for I learnt it when a child, and I believe I have not forgotten it." Gracious, imposing, practical, she was ever the great queen.

But her life was ebbing. When a favorite cousin died, she grew melancholy. She complained of cold in her legs. There was "a notable decay in her judgment," Robert Cecil reported. "She rests ill at nights, forbears to use the air in the day, and abstains more than usual from her meat."

She had refused to take medicine all her life, and none of the physicians who tended her could convince her to take any now. She grew weaker. As rumors of her mortal illness spread, directives for keeping the kingdom in order went out. And the country waited.

On March 19 her cousin Sir Robert Carey called on her. As he reported in his memoirs, he "found her in one of her withdrawing chambers, sitting low on her cushions." She said to him, "No, Robin, I am not well . . . . They have yoked my neck; I have no one whom I can trust. My condition is strangely turned upside down." On March 22, at the insistence of the Lord Admiral—and perhaps because of her own wretchedness—she confined herself to bed.

Now the members of her council visited her in earnest, trying to persuade her to name a successor. She knew, of course, that Cecil and others had been in regular commu-

Francis Bacon, a close adviser to Essex, won knighthood from King James. Bacon's works have earned him the lasting fame he yearned for as a statesman. Some people even believe he wrote the plays attributed to William Shakespeare.

nication with James VI of Scotland, and she too had had some correspondence with him in recent years. She knew he would succeed her, but still she refused to utter the confirming words.

On March 23 her speech failed. When the clergy came to her bedside, she followed their prayers mutely, pressing the archbishop's hand. When, once more, her councilors asked if her choice fell on James, she suddenly raised her arms out of bed and held them over her head in the form of a crown. Thus the succession of James was affirmed.

Before midday of March 24, Elizabeth was dead. By nightfall there were bonfires in the streets of London, and Sir Robert Carey was upon the Great North Road, riding to Edinburgh with the news. All over the country people were shouting "The Queen is dead; long live the King." A month later James VI of Scotland, aged thirty-seven, the Protestant son of Mary Queen of Scots, embarked on a slow, triumphal progress southward to be crowned James I of England.

As he moved toward London, all England wondered what to make of him. Men speculated on how he would affect England's political and social life, and how he would maintain the precarious religious balance between Protestants and Catholics. The actors, whose profession had been brought so high by Elizabeth's fond regard, may have wondered what restrictions the new monarch might impose.

Along the road from Scotland, James was entertained lavishly in the great houses he passed. And in the market towns he entered, throngs of people gathered to catch a glimpse of their king. He was not accustomed to such acclaim, such enthusiasm, such flattery. He was shrewd and intelligent, but at times he preferred hunting to tending the affairs of state. After years of studying the science of politics, he regarded himself as an able scholar and theorist. And he assumed he could use his knowledge to rule England effectively. He proved, however, to have more learning than understanding, for he failed to comprehend the gradual democratization of England that had been taking place during Elizabeth's long reign.

On May 7, 1603, London's civil authorities arrayed themselves on the road to the city to welcome James. With them was a crush of spectators whose enthusiasm reflected hope for their new monarch's successful reign, and relief that the question of the succession had been settled so peaceably. For all of them, life under James would be different. He lacked Elizabeth's grandeur; nor did he possess

While musicians play on the upper level, dancers perform on a stage set built to convey a feeling of great depth. This type of design, imported from Italy, was used in court entertainments during the reigns of Elizabeth and James.

her great love of and sympathy for England. Actually, all Elizabeth and James had in common was that the mother of each had been beheaded.

Two of Elizabeth's ministers became James' close advisers, and it was said that at first he was almost completely in their skillful hands. The men were Robert Cecil and his cousin Francis Bacon. Sir Walter Raleigh, who had hoped to become an influential personage in the new court, was excluded almost immediately. Cecil spoke critically of Raleigh to James, and the King received Raleigh coldly. Upon their meeting, James supposedly greeted him with a frosty pun, "I have heard *rawly* of thee."

A bitter sequence of events followed for Raleigh, for the King would heed none of his counsel. James wished to make peace with Spain. Raleigh, a fighter and a man who knew Spain very well, did not think it safe to do so. Raleigh believed that England's security could be assured only by maintaining a strong navy; James gave little thought to his or any country's supremacy on the high seas. He neglected the navy, and within a year of his ac-

After James' accession, as court performances became more elaborate, Shakespeare's company began acting before painted sets. The design at right was drawn by Inigo Jones for a production of Ben Jonson's Oberon *in 1611. Jones, a noted architect, brought to England the proscenium arch—the frame-like opening through which the stage is viewed in most modern theatres.*

Conspirators in the unsuccessful Gunpowder Plot were dragged to a gallows set up in the street, and publicly executed. In England, as on the Continent, executions were considered a form of entertainment.

cession, he had signed a treaty of peace with Spain.

Raleigh was never a man to keep his dissatisfaction quiet, and James was not a king to tolerate contrary opinions. In a series of swift steps, Raleigh was demoted, removed from his great house, and accused of treason. After a brief hearing, he was convicted and sentenced to die, but his execution was stayed and then postponed indefinitely. He remained a prisoner in the Tower for thirteen years before obtaining his release. After a short term of service abroad—a venture that ended disastrously—he was finally executed under his old sentence in 1618.

If James' treatment of Raleigh was unjust, his handling of religious affairs was even more unreasonable. The Catholics, who had been persecuted by previous English monarchs, were beginning to emerge from their underground status and demand greater tolerance. Fearful of growing Catholic strength, James would not risk acceding to their demands. Instead, he tightened religious restrictions, and Catholic resistance boiled over into violence with the infamous Gunpowder Plot of November, 1605.

The leader of this plot was a Catholic convert named Guy Fawkes, who had served in the Spanish army for a number of years. He and his fellow plotters worked for many months on a plan that would destroy the King and the Parliament as well. They intended to use barrels of gunpowder to blow up the Parliament buildings at a time when King James was addressing the members.

Preparations went smoothly, but several days before the explosion was to occur, word of the plot leaked out. The conspirators were arrested and eight of them were put to death on an outdoor scaffold erected opposite the houses of Parliament. The threat of violence had produced violent countermeasures. Had Elizabeth been alive, however, the offenders might have been pardoned, for she was skilled in the art of compromise. But James startled the nation by the sensational execution of the plotters.

If James had followed a similarly harsh policy toward the theatre, and if he had listened to his puritanical advisers who urged him to outlaw the acting companies, Shakespeare and his fellow players would have had to seek a new livelihood. James did indeed have fixed opinions regarding the theatre, but fortunately these ideas were favorable. Despite a strict upbringing that had cautioned him against playgoing, James had developed a lively and intelligent interest in the stage.

An Englishman named Lawrence Fletcher had been the monarch's favorite actor in Scotland. When James became king of England, he made certain that Fletcher joined a prominent London company, in this case the Lord Chamberlain's Men. With Fletcher's membership, the company received a new royal patent—and a new name, the King's Men. The patent was issued less than two weeks after James arrived in London. It made that group of actors—in which Shakespeare was still a sharer—the foremost company in all of England.

For a rather sober monarch James proved a surprisingly enthusiastic theatregoer. He saw, on the average, five times as many plays each year as Elizabeth had seen. More than half of these were presented by the King's Men. In addition to royal protection, its members received royal livery: scarlet cloth for cloaks, crimson velvet for capes.

The theatre thrived under James I, but the production of plays was suspended early in his reign when once again the plague struck London. It had begun in the Southwark district across the Thames even before James' accession, and by midsummer, 1603, it had broken out in the city with all its fury. Plague orders were issued, and the theatres were closed.

The King's Men embarked on a tour that lasted several months. Early in December they performed for King James at Wilton House, the Earl of Pembroke's home in Wiltshire. Later, during the Christmas season, the players entertained their sovereign—now also their patron—at Hampton Court.

After nearly a year the plague danger subsided, and the King's Men reopened the Globe on Easter Monday, 1604. Little over a year later, the company produced a play that many people believe Shakespeare wrote especially for King James. *Macbeth* was inspired by an old story about a Scottish king that Shakespeare had found in Holinshed's *Chronicles*, the source of so many of his plays. James was enthralled. Because of his Scottish birth, he was inclined to like the play. But he was also fascinated by its consideration of the powers of witchcraft. He had once written about demonology, and like many Englishmen of that time believed to some extent in the black arts.

Shakespeare had pleased his sovereign. Born in the age of Elizabeth, the playwright had made a smooth transition into the Jacobean age. Shakespeare's reputation had been established while Elizabeth was queen, but he would write some of his greatest plays—including *Othello* and *King Lear* —during the reign of James I.

The plot of Shakespeare's Macbeth *was taken from a tale of two Scottish captains who heard weird prophecies from three witches they met on the road one day (left).*

James' fear of swords—a carryover from childhood—was so great he constantly wore padded clothing to protect his person. His robes seem extra thick in this portrait by Daniel Mytens, a Dutch artist who was a court painter in England.

James did not alter the Crown's attitude toward the theatre. Yet, unlike his predecessor, he was quite concilia-tory toward Spain. At a table set with an elegant cloth, English and Spanish statesmen met in London's Somerset

House in 1604 to sign a treaty. The Spaniards are on the left of this portrait attributed to Marcus Gheeraerts. Among the English councilors on the right are Robert Cecil (far right) and the Lord Admiral (fourth from right).

132

VII

THE FIRST FOLIO

In 1609 an English vessel was wrecked on Bermuda. Accounts by survivors described how the terrified crew spent ten months on an island that they thought was inhabited by spirits. Details of the incident were so engrossing that Shakespeare became interested in the story. A year later he was at work on what turned out to be his most beautiful play, *The Tempest.* Called a comedy, it concerned a group of people shipwrecked in a storm. They were marooned and forced to stay on an enchanted island. During that time they were involved in a number of strange happenings caused by Prospero, a magician who could summon storms and make people appear and vanish at will.

Because of its many stage tricks and scenic effects, *The Tempest* was a challenge to its producers. It called for extraordinarily skilled actors, for it contained dialogue that was sometimes melodic, sometimes bombastic, and consistently exciting. The play was a significant addition to the catalogue of Shakespeare's plays (see page 149). Later he may have collaborated on other works, but *The Tempest* was probably the last play written entirely by Shakespeare. It was chosen to open the royal Christmas season at Whitehall Palace in 1611.

Shakespeare was forty-seven that year. As an actor and a playwright he had worked in the theatre for more than twenty years. Now, having gained wealth as well as a considerable reputation, he made plans for retirement. New Place, his home in Stratford, seemed ideal for the secluded life a retired gentleman might seek. Set on an acre of land, with two barns and two orchards, it had been

A colorful garden is nearly all that remains of New Place, Shakespeare's Stratford residence. After he retired there in 1611, he collaborated on at least one play, Henry VIII. *In the above scene from the play, Cardinal Wolsey is aghast as Henry shows him papers that will destroy his power.*

referred to for many years by townspeople as the Great House. It had a frontage of sixty feet, and it looked out on the graceful Guild Chapel and the old school that Shakespeare had attended many years before.

Stratford had changed considerably since Shakespeare's boyhood. It had gradually turned into a Puritan community. Whereas the acting companies had once been welcome, the Stratford council now banned the performance of plays in the town hall and threatened to fine any council member who licensed actors.

Despite these sober attitudes, which he must have found disagreeable, Shakespeare spent much of his time in Stratford after 1611. But he did not abandon London completely. In 1613, according to records, he purchased a house in the fashionable Blackfriars district—either as a part-time residence or more likely as an investment.

That year a play was produced that many people believe Shakespeare had a hand in. The work was performed under the title *All is True*, but it later became known as *Henry VIII*. It was first performed at the Globe on June 29, 1613. One of the key moments of the first act—the entrance of the king—was heralded by cannon fire. This was not an unusual stage effect, for cannons had been fired from the roofs of London theatres for many years. On that day, however, the discharge stopped the show. The thatch on the south side of the roof was ignited, and after smoldering for a while, burst into flame. In less than two hours, the Globe was a pile of rubble and charred debris.

Surprisingly, there were no casualties; the audience must have abandoned the theatre in an orderly fashion, without panic. There were a number of incidents, however —stories that were later told and retold by Londoners. One such tale concerned the gentleman in the Globe audience whose breeches caught fire, and who, with great presence of mind, put out the fire with a bottle of ale.

The Globe was soon rebuilt, for its owners were among the wealthiest actors in London. Shakespeare owned a share of the new theatre that reopened in 1614, but it is likely that by then he was spending most of his days in Stratford. His life had become that of a country gentleman surrounded by family and friends. There was his wife, his sister, his younger daughter Judith, and Susanna, his older daughter. Some years earlier, Susanna had married a distinguished physician, Dr. John Hall.

Shakespeare had little to do with local affairs, but he enjoyed the company of his fellow townsmen. He also

The last play Shakespeare wrote as an actor in London was The Tempest, *first performed in 1611.*

134

played host to prominent literary figures who came to New Place to visit him—men like Ben Jonson and the poet Michael Drayton. A Stratford vicar, too young to have known Shakespeare, but acquainted with the playwright's nephews and with surviving Stratfordians, later recalled one of Shakespeare's gatherings. It had taken place early in March, 1616. According to the vicar, "Shakespeare, Drayton, and Ben Jonson had a merry meeting, and it seems, drank too hard, for Shakespeare died of a fever there contracted."

It is probably not true that a reunion with other authors from his London days brought on Shakespeare's final

A portrait of Shakespeare engraved by Martin Droeshout is on the title page of the First Folio (below). A foreword by Ben Jonson, referring to "gentle Shakespeare," faces it.

To the Reader.

This Figure, that thou here seest put,
It was for gentle Shakespeare cut;
Wherein the Grauer had a strife
with Nature, to out-doo the life:
O, could he but haue drawne his wit
As well in brasse, as he hath hit
His face; the Print would then surpasse
All, that vvas euer vvrit in brasse.
But, since he cannot, Reader, looke
Not on his Picture, but his Booke.

B. I.

Mr. WILLIAM
SHAKESPEARES
COMEDIES,
HISTORIES, &
TRAGEDIES.
Published according to the True Originall Copies.

LONDON
Printed by Isaac Iaggard, and Ed. Blount. 1623.

Belching smoke and flame, like this contemporary field piece, a cannon set the Globe's roof afire. In two hours the playhouse was destroyed.

illness. Yet is is difficult to piece together from available evidence the cause of his death—or to discern what final thoughts were on his mind. Apparently he was ill by March 25. There was on that day a hurried attempt by Shakespeare's lawyer to make necessary, last-minute revisions in the playwright's will. The haste involved in making these changes was probably caused by the lawyer's desire to put all his client's affairs in good order before it was too late.

The will that Shakespeare had drawn up earlier in the year mentioned his daughter Judith as a spinster—since then she had married, but she had not married well. Shakespeare wanted to make sure she and her children would be cared for, but he also wanted to prevent his disreputable son-in-law from inheriting his money. As the bequests to Judith appeared on the first page of the will, the entire document did not have to be revised. The lawyer's clerk merely crossed out lines, and in his fine, small hand, wrote in additions at the bottom of the page (see page 141).

The will remained in draft form and was filed with the town clerk. But was the will not recopied because Shakespeare was so ill that a delay could not be risked? Probably; he had only a month to live. If the lawyer had chosen the more careful way and had had a "fair" copy of the will drawn up, modern researchers would have been denied this intimate glimpse of Shakespeare, suddenly concerned about family problems as his time to die drew near.

Although it was not particularly neat, Shakespeare's will was wholly legal. He had put his signature on each page—"By me, William Shakespeare"—and it appears more or less in the same form as on earlier documents. But, except for the alterations, the document is a strangely unrevealing one. Unlike the wills of his contemporaries, it is impersonal, containing few descriptive adjectives and thus giving no indication of Shakespeare's feelings toward his family or friends.

According to the inscription on his tombstone, he died on April 23, 1616, and according to parish records he was buried two days later inside the chancel of the Church of the Holy Trinity in Stratford. The great bell in the tower of the Guild Chapel tolled as Shakespeare's wooden coffin was lowered to its resting place. The inscription, which Shakespeare may have written or selected himself, was carved on a flagstone over the grave:

> Good friend, for Jesus' sake, forbear,
> To dig the dust enclosed here:
> Blest be the man that spares these stones,
> And curst be he that moves my bones.

The spot was marked with a bust commissioned by Shakespeare's more prosperous son-in-law, Dr. Hall, and sculpted by a monument maker of London, Geraert Janssen. It is believed to be a good likeness of the playwright, even though the rendering itself was somewhat crude. Apparently, detailed carving was beyond the skill of the artist. Most of the features and high lights were brought out with

This was probably the first drawing made to illustrate a play by Shakespeare. Drawn in 1594, it represents a scene in act one of Titus Andronicus: *Tamora begs Titus to spare her son's life.*

Stratford's tallest, most imposing structure is the Church of the Holy Trinity. Its stone spire pierces the sky above ancient elm trees in the picture at left. Shakespeare lies buried in the chancel of this church. Behind his tomb, recessed in the wall, is a monument with a bust of the playwright (right) that was sculpted by Geraert Janssen.

paint and brush. It was colorful but uninspired, a studied pose of the playwright with pen and paper in hand, staring blankly into eternity.

To Shakespeare's friends, the immediate problem was how best to memorialize the great playwright. By 1619, with the death of Richard Burbage, only two members of the original Lord Chamberlain's company were left: John Heminges and Henry Condell. These two actors took on the responsibility of gathering and preserving the body of Shakespeare's work. Both of them were intimately acquainted with Shakespeare's writings and were probably best qualified to judge which of the many plays attributed to him were actually his. They approached their great task as a labor of love, stating:

We have but collected them [the plays] and done an office to the dead to procure his orphans guardians; without ambition either of self-profit or fame; only to keep the memory of so worthy a friend and fellow alive as was our Shakespeare . . .

It was a painstaking job they undertook because so many of the original manuscripts had been lost. Heminges and Condell shunned the printed texts of the plays in many cases, for these were inaccurate and distorted. When manuscripts were unavailable, the two men devoted much time to unearthing prompters' versions, which had been copied from the author's original work. In some instances, however, they had to sift through stacks of garbled editions, probing their memories to determine how Shakespeare's language had been mutilated, and then attempt to restore his words.

Printing plays in folio form, that is, in one single volume, was a costly enterprise; only Ben Jonson had attempted it. Heminges and Condell had difficulty finding a printer willing to risk publishing the thirty-six plays they had collected. At the time of his death, Shakespeare's reputation was not nearly so great as Jonson's, and Jonson's folio had not sold widely.

But the actors persevered, and they found a printer who agreed to take on the task—and the risk. The first folio of plays by William Shakespeare was printed, and on November 8, 1623, was entered in the Stationers' Register. Jonson wrote a long poetic eulogy for the folio, and a commercial artist named Martin Droeshout was engaged to provide a drawing for the title page. His copperplate engraving, and the bust that stands in the Stratford church, are thought to be the only Shakespeare portraits with any real basis in life. The playwright's widow, Anne, was still living at the time; it is believed that she saw and approved them both.

In 1740 another significant statuary portrait of Shakespeare was fashioned. It was placed in the famed Poets' Corner of Westminster Abbey in London. But neither this portrait nor any of the others do justice to the man himself or to his memory. His published plays keep his memory alive more effectively than stone or canvas. For as long as there are actors to read his lines, Shakespeare will be a vital, living force in the theatre.

The words Ben Jonson wrote for inclusion in the First Folio were flattering indeed, although somewhat conventional in their patriotic pride. He wrote: "Triumph, my Britain! Thou hast one to show To whom all scenes of Europe homage owe." But Jonson crowned his tribute to William Shakespeare with a line that was surely as heartfelt as it is accurate: "He was not of an age, but for all time."

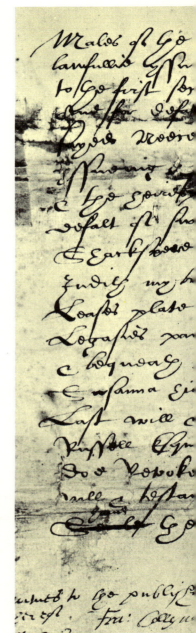

The last page of Shakespeare's will contains this entry, scrawled almost illegibly over the ninth line: "Item, I gyve unto my wief my second best bed with the furniture." The will, with changes and deletions, was written out by a legal clerk, and Shakespeare's signature is visible on every page.

THE MEMORIAL THEATRES

William Shakespeare has long been considered the world's out-
standing playwright; but never in history have his plays been
so applauded as today. Part of the reason for this extraordi-
nary popularity is the availability of good editions of his works
—the legacy of Heminges and Condell, who first compiled the
plays. A weightier reason for Shakespeare's popularity is the
recent construction of several theatres in which his plays can
be seen to best advantage. The first of these to be built was
the Royal Shakespeare Theatre in Stratford, England (right).
This plain but highly efficient playhouse, which opened in
1932, has an extended stage on three sides of which members
of the ground-floor audience are seated. The theatre, visited
by more than 250,000 playgoers each year, rises above the
Avon like a no-nonsense palace, and near it on the riverbank
stands the Gower memorial statue of Shakespeare (below). The
playwright broods atop a column, surrounded by sculptures of
various characters from his plays (visible here is an athletic
Henry V, holding high the crown of England). On the following pages are other memorial theatres, noteworthy both for
their excellent stages and for their other crowd-pleasing features, which are contributing to Shakespeare's new popularity.

Directors of the handsomely decorated Shakespeare theatre in Stratford, Connecticut, encourage crowds (200,000 annually) to picnic on the grass before the performances.

Of all the new Shakespeare theatres, the playhouse in Stratford, Ontario, has the most modern equipment. At left players act The Comedy of Errors *on an extended stage.*

One of the newest Shakespeare theatres is located in New York City's Central Park. Here, during an eve-

...ing performance of The Tempest, *actors wave a sheet before a balcony "ship" to simulate stormy seas.*

The caricaturist George Cruikshank etched this illustration of Sir John Falstaff; the artist gave credit to the true creator of the character by the line "Drawn by William Shakespeare."

HOW OLD IS FALSTAFF?

There can be little doubt about when Shakespeare's knavish knight Sir John Falstaff was born—1597. He came to life in that year on the stage of the Globe Theatre in *Henry IV, Part One*, and Londoners immediately took him to their hearts. With other Shakespearean characters the problem is far more difficult, however, for the dates of first performances of plays in which they appear are uncertain. For example, Berowne, the mocking lover in *Love's Labour's Lost*, saw the light of day for the first time either in 1592, when some scholars believe the play was given at Hampton Court, or in 1594, a date preferred by others. Thus the list below, Shakespeare's plays arranged in order of their performance date, represents the best possible approximation—not a final answer. The list was assembled by Professor Gerald Eades Bentley of Princeton University for his book *Shakespeare: A Biographical Handbook.*

Henry VI, Part Two—1590–91
Henry VI, Part Three—1590–91
Henry VI, Part One—1591–92
Richard III—1592–93
The Comedy of Errors—1592–93
Titus Andronicus—1593–94
Taming of the Shrew—1593–94
Two Gentlemen of Verona—1594–95
Love's Labour's Lost—1594–95
Romeo and Juliet—1594–95
Richard II—1595–96
A Midsummer Night's Dream—1595–96
King John—1596–97
The Merchant of Venice—1596–97
Henry IV, Part One—1597–98
Henry IV, Part Two—1597–98
Much Ado About Nothing—1598–99
Henry V—1598–99
Julius Caesar—1599–1600

As You Like It—1599–1600
Twelfth Night—1599–1600
Hamlet—1600–1601
The Merry Wives of Windsor—1600–1601
Troilus and Cressida—1601–2
All's Well That Ends Well—1602–3
Measure for Measure—1604–5
Othello—1604–5
King Lear—1605–6
Macbeth—1605–6
Antony and Cleopatra—1606–7
Coriolanus—1607–8
Timon of Athens—1607–8
Pericles—1608–9
Cymbeline—1609–10
The Winter's Tale—1610–11
The Tempest—1611–12
Henry VIII—1612–13
The Two Noble Kinsmen—1612–13

Elizabeth, enthroned opposite the letter "B" in this woodcut, is entertained at a water pageant whose components include a floating castle and a school of sea nymphs.

AMERICAN HERITAGE PUBLISHING CO., INC.

James Parton, *President*

Joseph J. Thorndike, Jr., *Editorial Director*

Richard M. Ketchum, *Editor, Book Division*

Irwin Glusker, *Art Director*

HORIZON CARAVEL BOOKS

RUSSELL BOURNE, *Managing Editor*

Janet Czarnetzki, *Art Director*

Mervyn Kaufman, *Associate Editor*

Judith Harkison, *Chief Picture Researcher*

Lucy Davidson Rosenfeld, *Picture Researcher*

Elaine K. Andrews, *Copy Editor*

Mary Gloyne Payne, *Editorial Assistant*

Nancy Simon, *Editorial Assistant*

Gertrudis Feliu, *Chief, European Bureau*

Susanne Puddefoot, *London*

ACKNOWLEDGMENTS

The Editors would like to express their appreciation to the staff members of many private and public collections in which paintings, photographs, and articles of special importance to this book were found. Foremost among these collections are the British Museum, the National Portrait Gallery, the Victoria and Albert Museum, and the British Travel & Holidays Association, London; the Bodleian Library, Oxford; the New York Public Library; and the Folger Shakespeare Library, Washington, D.C. In addition, the Editors wish to thank the following individuals and organizations for their assistance and for making available material in their collections:

Manuscript Department, Department of Printed Books, Department of Prints and Drawings—British Museum

Caroline Cole, Mary Hewes, Margaret Jochem, Virginia LaMar, and Julia Peacock—Folger Shakespeare Library

Elizabeth Roth, Wilson Duprey—Prints Division, New York Public Library

Levi Fox—Director, The Shakespeare Birthplace Trust, Stratford on Avon

R. Holmes—Assistant Keeper, London Museum

David T. Piper—Assistant Keeper, National Portrait Gallery, London

Frank de Heyman—Brooklyn, New York

Irwin Smith—Garden City, New York

Special research and photography: England—Archive Research Ltd., Zoltan Wegner, John R. Freeman, Derek Bayes, Photographic Studios of the British Museum; Italy—Maria Todorow; Washington, D.C.—Charles Baptie; New York—Geoffrey Clements

FURTHER REFERENCE

Examples of Elizabethan furniture and art can be found in the collections of most major museums in the United States. Some of these are The Metropolitan Museum of Art, New York; the Folger Shakespeare Library and the National Gallery of Art, Washington, D.C.; the Museum of Fine Arts, Boston; the Philadelphia Museum of Art; and the M.H. de Young Memorial Museum, San Francisco. However, the most complete collections are located in England in the following museums: the British Museum, the National Portrait Gallery, the London Museum, and the Victoria and Albert Museum, London.

For those who wish to read further on Shakespeare and Elizabethan England, the following books are recommended:

Adams, Joseph Quincy. *A Life of William Shakespeare*. Houghton Mifflin, 1925.

Beckerman, Bernard. *Shakespeare at the Globe*. Macmillan, 1962.

Bentley, Gerald Eades. *Shakespeare: A Biographical Handbook*. Yale University Press, 1961.

Black, J. B. *The Reign of Elizabeth: 1558–1603*. Clarendon Press, 1959.

Burton, Elizabeth. *The Pageant of Stuart England*. Scribner's, 1962.

Chambers, E. K. *William Shakespeare: A Study of Facts and Problems*. 2 vols. Clarendon Press, 1930.

Chute, Marchette. *An Introduction to Shakespeare*. E. P. Dutton, 1951.

Chute, Marchette. *Shakespeare of London*. E. P. Dutton, 1949.

Chute, Marchette. *Stories from Shakespeare*. World Publishing Co., 1956.

Dunlop, Ian. *Palaces and Progresses of Elizabeth I*. Jonathan Cape, 1962.

Halliday, F. E. *Shakespeare: A Pictorial Biography*. Thames and Hudson, 1956.

Halliday, F. E. *Shakespeare in His Age*. Gerald Duckworth & Co., 1956.

Harbage, Alfred. *Shakespeare's Audience*. Columbia University Press, 1961.

Harrison, David. *Tudor England*. 2 vols. Cassell and Co., 1953.

Irwin, Margaret. *Elizabeth, Captive Princess*. Harcourt, 1948.

Irwin, Margaret. *Young Bess*. Harcourt, 1944.

Jenkins, Elizabeth. *Elizabeth and Leicester*. Coward-McCann, 1961.

Jenkins, Elizabeth. *Elizabeth the Great*. Coward-McCann, 1958.

Nicoll, Allardyce. *The Elizabethans*. Cambridge University Press, 1957.

Ogburn, Charlton, Jr. and Dorothy. *Shake-speare: The Real Man Behind the Name*. William Morrow and Co., 1962.

Scott, Walter. *Kenilworth*. Collins Classics, 1959.

Strachey, Lytton. *Elizabeth and Essex*. Harcourt, 1928.

Summerson, John. *Architecture in Britain 1530–1830*. Penguin Books Ltd., 1953.

Wickham, Glynn. *Early English Stages*. Vol. I, 1959. Vol. II, 1963. Columbia University Press.

Wilson, E. P. *The Plague in Shakespeare's London*. Clarendon Press, 1927.

Wilson, John Dover. *Life in Shakespeare's England*. Penguin Books, 1962.

Wright, Louis B. and LaMar, Virginia A., Eds. *Life and Letters in Tudor and Stuart England*. Cornell University Press, 1962.

Wright, Louis B. and LaMar, Virginia A., Eds. *The Folger Library General Reader's Shakespeare*. 20 vols. (paperback), Washington Square Press, 1957 to date.

INDEX

Bold face indicates pages on which maps or illustrations appear

S. PAULES CHURCH

Cheapside Crosse

Three Cranes

The Stilliardt

The Gally fuste

Kell Schipes

THAMESIS

The Bear Gardne

The Globe

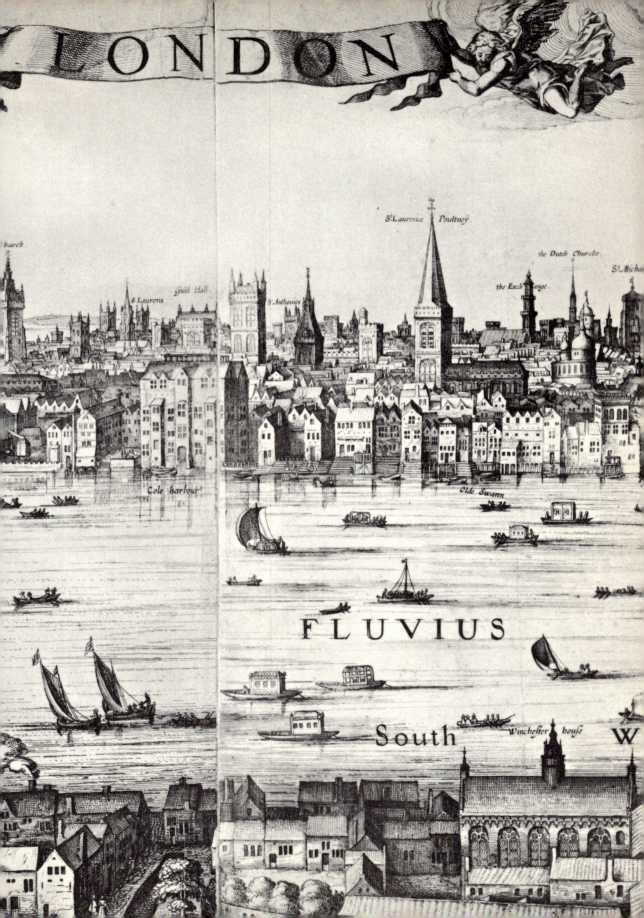

DATE DUE		